PARENTS GUIDE TO STUDENT SUCCESS

Home and School Partners in the Twenty-First Century

Irving H. Buchen

ScarecrowEducation
Lanham, Maryland • Toronto • Oxford
2004

Published in the United States of America
by ScarecrowEducation
An imprint of The Rowman & Littlefield Publishing Group, Inc.
4501 Forbes Boulevard, Suite 200, Lanham, Maryland 20706
www.scaroweducation.com

PO Box 317
Oxford
OX2 9RU, UK

British Library Cataloguing in Publication Information Available

Library of Congress Cataloging-in-Publication Data
Buchen, Irving H., 1930–
   Parents guide to student success : home and school partners in the
twenty-first century / Irving Buchen.
   p. cm.
   ISBN 1-57886-126-8 (pbk. : alk. paper)
   1. Education—Parent participation—United States. 2. Home and
school—United States. I. Title.
   LB1048.5.B83 2004
   371.19'2—dc22   2003027646

Dedicated to
our children, our grandchildren,
and the legacy of always new beginnings

CONTENTS

ACKNOWLEDGMENTS

Where to start? With my own parents of course and with my brothers and sister and all the many aunts and uncles, cousins, and friends who shaped me, especially my two boyhood friends, Harold Adelson and Gerry Leavitt, both of whom are godfathers to our youngest son, Elan. I dedicate this book to all our children and grandchildren and thank them for the many ways they have helped us to be parents.

But I need to acknowledge two seminal, original, and creative thinkers who have strongly influenced this book: William Glasser and Howard Gardner. In particular, I appreciate their responses to my many inquiries. I have borrowed extensively from both in my effort to stretch and apply their ideas to the issues of parents. I hope in the process I have not strayed from and been unfaithful to their basic concepts. If I have erred, the blame is mine.

INTRODUCTION

This book is not about childrearing; there are many good ones available. The focus here is not on raising but guiding kids—on what parents can do to help their kids be successful in school. But isn't that what parents have always done? Of course, but there are at least five new factors that make that process more different and difficult now than ever before:

1. Today's parents are different than their own parents.
2. Today's kids as students are a totally new breed.
3. Schooling and learning have changed dramatically.
4. More choices and more complex options are available.
5. Competition for educational opportunities is more intense.

Although each of the above will be examined in detail later, some general remarks may be in order here.

I. DIFFERENT PARENTS

In 1995, a survey of Ohio parents indicated that more than 60 percent believed public schools generally were doing an adequate job. But that level of support went up to 85 percent when receptivity to parental involvement was included.

Today's parents are what could be called the "Yes, but" generation. For the most part they believe that schools have done right by their kids, but—and here is where their approval, like those in Ohio, becomes conditional and includes an agenda of improvement—standards should be raised, classes should be smaller and safer, teaching should be more individualized, and above all parents should be welcomed and accepted as educational contributors and even partners. In short, the current generation of parents is not only more assertive, savvier, and smarter, but also insistent on playing a major role in both education in general and the educational development of their kids in particular. Sadly, that new role has not been sufficiently recognized and responded to by most educators. In fact, indirectly this book is intended as a wake-up call to schools.

2. YOUTH CULTURE

Today's sensational dress and body adornments are but the tip of the iceberg; the really telling differences are deeper. First, K–12 is essentially a technological culture. Their world is predominantly electronic; they are the first generation to be raised on computers. Second, advertising and marketing have programmed them into being outstanding consumers. Recently, two media companies created the cartoon characters of Big Red Dog and Care Bears to sell to preschool children. Third, kids are getting older faster. Girls and boys achieve sexual puberty at much earlier ages, and teenage pregnancies now start with eleven-to-twelve-year-olds.

3. SCHOOLS THEMSELVES ARE DIFFERENT

Some of the buildings may not have changed much, but what takes place inside has. First, schooling and learning are no longer synonymous. Educators generally, but especially parents, increasingly recognize that schools do not have a monopoly on knowledge acquisition. Then, too, teachers do not function in the same way. Complexity of approaches and performance monitoring require them to be as multitasked as many parents in order to administer the learning they teach. Above all, many schools have set up electronic links between school and home. Data is shared about attendance, homework, test dates, and so on, on a per child basis. Recently, Broward County in Florida introduced the Virtual Counselor, which makes available a student's total school record since kindergarten.

4. SCHOOL CHOICE

Historically, choices were limited. Students generally attended public schools; sixty million do so now. Or they attended parochial or religious schools—about ten million today. Or they enrolled in private, usually college prep, schools—about two million. Now in addition to those traditional options, kids can be homeschooled—about two million currently—or attend a charter school—the number of which is over 2,000 and growing. In addition, public schools in turn offer extensive internal choices at all levels—so much so that many schools have hired a separate administrator in charge of school choice. To compound the situation, many schools have become specialty schools or academies serving as magnet schools in the arts, sciences, or communications. Many parents now check out how many teachers are Golden Apple winners and how many are certified by the National Board of Teacher Standards at schools. (It has become a rehearsal like the later review of college faculties to determine where they earned their doctorates.) So armed, many parents elect to send their kids to certain magnet schools, even if the specialty does not fit in with the kid's career plans, because the quality of the instruction and stimulation are just too good to pass up.

A relatively recent development that is increasingly being tapped is the high school–college option. Students with a GPA of 3.0 in high school can take college-level courses, usually at the local community college, and receive both high school and college credit at no tuition cost. The net result is that some enterprising students are able to complete as much as the equivalent of the entire freshman year of college while still in high school. They not only earn a high school diploma at the same time, but also in the process save an entire year of college tuition. Finally, there are cyberschools, either totally electronic or blended with face-to-face instruction. Some states such as Florida have created a statewide virtual school, which can be tapped by students all around the state. Time trumps space.

5. COMPETITION

Traditionally, competition surfaced as an educational factor only during the senior year when college acceptance loomed large. In a few cities, it occurs earlier, at the end of middle school. Certain prestigious public high schools require for admission passing tough entrance exams, having a high GPA, and having glowing letters of recommendation. But formidable though these traditional hurdles were and still are, they are dwarfed by the across-the-board competition that now has accompanied school choice.

It starts as early as nursery school; many have waiting lists. Charter schools tend to be small in size and often acceptance is limited. In many school districts, choice is influenced by the expense of bussing, which has been shifted to parents. In some cases, families are asked to buy books and supplies. Above all, economics has forced many urban districts to close many small and underutilized neighborhood schools or to consolidate them to realize economies of scale. The same has happened in rural areas. Even community colleges and state universities have turned away qualified students because of reduced budgets and frozen the hiring of full-time professors in favor of lower-paid adjuncts. In short, access is no longer guaranteed and is increasingly driven by competition and choice, which in turn function and alternate as cause and effect.

In the past all parents sought the same goals: "Help my kids become smarter, happier, and responsible." That has not changed; what has is how it all happens. Because the obstacles are more formidable, the risks greater, and the choices more complex, parents have to change and adopt new and more proactive roles. They have had to become learning advocates and knowledge brokers for their offspring. In the process, planning has become a dominant parental mode. Even financial planning for college now is superseded and preceded by future projections that span pre-K–16 and that track a total educational developmental line.

The goal of this book is to help parents negotiate and navigate just such current educational complexities. Parents now not only have to rear their kids but also mentor them through the labyrinth of schooling and learning. To do that effectively and knowledgeably, they in turn need a mentor. Hopefully, this guide will serve that role and provide them with a fighting chance and an even playing field to be advocates for the future of their kids.

Part I

ORIENTATION TO THE BASICS

There are at least three basic reasons why parents have to change if they are to be effective champions of their kids and if their kids are to be successful learners in school, life, and work:

1. Education itself is changing drastically and will continue to do so during the entire growing period of your offspring. You have to know what is in store for them if you are to provide intelligent help and support. Indeed, the drivers of future educational change are so powerful, diverse, and invasive that subsequent to an assessment of the current national situation, I have added a final chapter on the future of education, 2005–2025.

2. The impact of education on some kids can be traumatic; the effects may last their lifetimes. Although children are resilient (only children can survive childhood—adults could not), parents need to take a preventative-medicine approach and bolster their formative years. If necessary, they should be ready to intervene and to fight to save their later years. Above all, they have to counteract school failure.

3. The research proves what many already knew: namely, that parents make a difference, often life-changing and life-sustaining.

But we have also learned more about that impact. For example, we have a better and even predictive sense of parental role changes and how they affect and can even turn around schools. We have more precise and reliable profiles of what different schools need from various parents' perspectives, in other words a more optimum matching process. We have a better idea of what obstacles exist within schools and within the psyche of parents that prevent or compromise effective parent involvement and how to overcome those hurdles. Finally, we are aware of the extent to which the contributions of parents to the new nationally mandated educational goals may be not only helpful but even indispensable to the achievement of those objectives.

All these orientations are the subjects of the first three chapters. How kids get started may determine how they finish. The same applies to why this book begins with the basics.

THE NEW NATIONAL MANDATE

Education is no longer a local matter. For better or worse, it is now national policy, federally regulated, prescribed, and mandated. In addition, it affects and applies across the board and covers the total span of education, K–12 (in some states pre-K–16).

It has a brief history. For many years, educators and especially politicians sensitive to U.S. standings around the world argued for the kind of national curriculum that a number of advanced countries had, but no agreement was ever reached on what it should contain, and the cause failed to gather support. By the beginning of this century, the issue was revived, but this time the decision was to shift from a national curriculum and opt for the next best thing: national standards. And so from 2001–2002, new education authorization legislation became the law of the land. It is called No Child Left Behind (NCLB) and was signed into law on January 8, 2002. From the perspective of this book and of parents in general, the legislation also could have been called No Parent Left Out.

To appreciate the nearly total coverage and application of NCLB, consider the following dimensions of compliance:

- Every state and every state department of education is required to submit to the federal Department of Education a state plan of how its educational requirements and proficiencies will be met according to mandated precise timetables.

- Every school district in turn must submit its plans for compliance and be aligned to the state plan.
- Every school must do the same.
- Every teacher in every classroom must mirror the school plan.
- Every student will be required to evidence "adequate yearly progress."
- Every school district and state will develop parental involvement programs with direct input from and agreement with parents.
- In the event schools fall into categories of needing improvement, corrective action, or restructuring, there are a number of options that must be given to parents.

So the first thing parents have to recognize is that education is now a new ball game, and the rules apply nationally. Moving to another part of the state or even to another state won't change anything, but the rules do not apply to private or parochial schools and that may affect their enrollments. However, what is abundantly clear is that if parents are to help steer their kids through the labyrinth of education, they had best know more about the national standards of NCLB and, specifically, what it requires of districts, schools, individual teachers, and students. Forewarned is forearmed.

Other than the extent of the compliance noted above, NCLB has a number of additional major sections and applications.

FUNDING

- Financial support for over 90 percent of school districts comes from over forty federal programs covered by NCLB.
- Of the nine titles or sections of NCLB, Title I and II are the largest programs.
- More than 47,000 schools receive Title I funds and extra academic support for low-income children. These include before- and after-school programs, family literacy and parenting classes, libraries, technology, and safe and drug-free schools.

- All school districts are eligible for funds from Title II.
- Title II funds focus on school personnel: training, recruiting and retaining teachers, administrators, and paraprofessionals.
- Lack of compliance can result in the loss of these funds.

GOALS

- Increase performance by raising standards.
- Have standards in place for all students in reading and math by 2002–2003.
- Every student will achieve proficiency by 2013–2014.
- Every state will develop standards, assessment systems, and accountability measures to achieve the goal of no child left behind.
- All teachers, administrators, and paraprofessionals must not only be licensed but highly qualified.
- An annual report card on the performance of each school will be compiled and published.
- Rewards will be provided for schools that meet or exceed academic goals.
- Schools that fall behind will be officially and publicly identified as such.
- Such schools will fall into one of three categories: needing improvement, corrective action, or restructuring.
- Parents will be notified of such performance judgments and what options and choices they can exercise accordingly.

CALENDAR AND TIMETABLE

- NCLB is basically driven by standards and the testing process that embodies those standards.
- By 2002–2003, all standards for reading and math should be in place.
- By 2005–2006, every state will test every child every year in reading and math in grades 3–8. Both tests also will be given in grades 10–12.
- By 2005–2006, science standards should be in place.

- By 2007–2008, every student will be tested in science at least once in grades 3–5, 6–9, and 10–12.
- By 2013–2014, all students in every school in every state will have achieved a level of educational proficiency in reading, math, and science.
- Every year a performance report card for every school shall be issued to parents.

CATEGORIES OF DEFICIENCY AND SCHOOL CONSEQUENCES

- The key measure of performance is annual yearly progress (AYP).
- Three designations apply.
- After putting in place testing against standards, if a school fails to achieve AYP overall for two consecutive years, it is dubbed as needing improvement.
- No AYP for three years results in a school being subject to corrective action.
- No AYP for four to five consecutive years results in the school being restructured or taken over by the state.

PARENTAL OPTIONS

- All school districts are now required by law to inform parents as to the performance status of the schools their kids attend and what their action options are.
- For schools designated as needing improvement, parents can transfer their children to another public or charter school that is not on the list of poorly performing schools. In addition, the district must pay for costs of bus transportation.
- In addition, schools needing improvement must establish a team of parents and community representatives to develop a plan to improve the school.
- For schools designated in need of corrective action, parents, in addition to the transfer option, can select a supplemental additional service provider or tutoring service to provide after-school help.

- Such schools will also be required to go through extensive restructuring, which includes replacing existing administrators, teachers, and staff.
- If there is no AYP for five consecutive years, in addition to providing public school choice and supplemental services for children, the school may be taken over by the state or turned over to a private for-profit educational management company.
- For states with voucher programs, parents can include enrolling students in private or parochial schools as part of their choice. A voucher program has been approved by Congress for the District of Columbia. If it succeeds, it may be followed by a national voucher plan incorporated into existing NCLB legislation.

NEW ROLES OF PARENTS

The new legislation offers parents not only a greater say in the education of their children, but also a greater series of empowered roles directing their education. In particular three distinct but progressively inclusive roles have surfaced: Involvement, Partnership, and Leadership.

Involvement

This is the most traditional and familiar role, except now two new dimensions are involved. First, parental involvement is not an option; it is mandated; and parents are not left in the dark but given the information and data of periodic report cards to guide their involvement. Second, the process cannot be piecemeal. Current legislation requires the coordination of all current parent involvement programs. That includes all federal programs, such as Even Start, Head Start, Early Reading First, Transition from Preschool to Kindergarten, and so on.

Partnership

In many ways the school and the home always have been partners. Now, however, partnership is both required and specified. The new form it is to take is a compact, which is a written agreement between teachers and parents. It is be signed by all parents of Title I students and countersigned by their teachers.

In language that parents can understand, the following is to be spelled out and made part of the compact:

- The academic expectations and goals for each child.
- The strategies that will be used to achieve those goals.
- The means and timetable to measure progress.
- The student's assets and learning needs.
- The cooperative support available from parents and home to help achieve adequate yearly progress to goal achievement.

Ideally, such mutual understanding should have been in place. Now at least that ideal is real and required.

Leadership

Leadership initiatives involve direct participation in parent involvement teams working with schools, districts, and state departments of education and maintaining open and full communication channels with all education officials and entities. Of the two the second is the more difficult and important.

Historically, schools and school districts have not shared information with or been particularly accommodating to parents' requests for changes. Such old habits die hard; old cultures even more so. So the brunt of parental leadership will fall on pushing for parents' right to know. According to the legislation, every school district receiving Title I funds is required at the beginning of every school year to respond to parental requests about the qualifications of their children's teachers and paraprofessionals. However, following the good advice of the National PTA, parent leaders should push the information-gathering process further to include minimally the answers to the following questions:

- What are the qualifications of the teachers of my kids?
- How many teachers in the school are highly qualified?
- How many are not teaching in their field of expertise?

- What about the new teachers hired? Are all highly qualified? If not, why not?
- For teachers who are not highly qualified, what is your plan to bring them to that level? By what date?
- Are we facing a teacher shortage? What are you doing to offset that?
- What is the retention rate of good teachers? If we are losing many, and especially good ones, do we know why, and what it would take to keep them?

PARENTS' RIGHTS

One can become so preoccupied with current legislation and an examination of its future impacts that a very basic piece of older legislation can be overlooked. It is called The Family Education Rights and Privacy Act, sometimes called the Buckley Amendment, which was passed by Congress in 1974. Although it is still on the books and the law of the land, it is generally unknown to parents and not eagerly or openly advertised by school officials.

The Act guarantees the following parents' rights of access:

1. The right to all information and materials maintained by the school on your child, regardless of format or location of such records.
2. The right to challenge information in the record.
3. The right to correct what is recorded.
4. The right to determine who other than school personnel has the right to access your child's record.
5. The right to require parental consent before releasing your child's record for any but educational uses or purposes, and to anyone other than school personnel.

To appreciate fully what this act offers parents and to employ direct and clear non-legalese language, here are some the key questions parents typically ask:

Q. What does PRC or PRT stand for?
A. Permanent Record Card or File.

Q. *Why is it called permanent and what does it usually contain?*

A. It is called permanent because it travels with and covers all the students' basic activities in all grades and subjects throughout all their years in the district. If the student transfers to another district, the PRC accompanies the student. Minimally, it contains:

- report cards.
- medical records.
- standardized test scores.
- psychological tests.
- attendance records.
- evaluations for gifted or special programs.
- referrals to other programs.

Q. *Does the Buckley Amendment define what information is to be included or not included in the PRC?*

A. No. It only guarantees your right of access, but it does not give you the right to see the personal notes of the school staff unless they are made part of the permanent record or appear in the records of other children. However, you have the right to challenge any scores or information you do not understand and to have those explained to you in simple and nontechnical language.

Q. *How often should parents review records?*

A. At least once a year, especially before a parent–teacher conference. It is also a good idea to inspect the record after a discipline or academic problem. Above all, make sure the record is examined if the student is changing schools or school districts.

Q. *Can the school refuse access?*

A. No, they have forty-five days to comply. During that time the school cannot destroy, remove, or alter any materials in the file.

Q. *What can legitimately be challenged?*

A. Items that are misleading, discriminatory, inaccurate, or that violate your privacy or that of your child. There should be no personal comments relating to you, your family, or your child. Some local PTAs maintain a list of parents who are particularly experienced in the process and who can accompany or advise parents.

Q. *What is the procedure to follow in correcting records or expunging information?*

A. Usually the school asks or requires the parental request to be in writing. In most cases that goes to the principal and it is resolved at that level. If he refuses to accede to your request, you have the right to request a hearing with the hearing officer of the school district. Regardless of the outcome you have the right to have your written request placed in your child's permanent record.

Q. *What usually happens?*

A. Most principals have been trained in school law and will provide access and correct or delete what is not appropriate. Extensive delay may indicate that something inappropriate has taken place; if access is denied or a child's records have been released without parental consent, a written complaint should be mailed to: Family Policy and Regulation Office, Department of Education, 400 Maryland Ave. SW, Room 3021, Washington, D.C. 20202-4605. A copy of that complaint should also be sent to the school board. That will probably result in a rapid response.

Clearly, parents are not without their rights, but only if they are aware of and exercise them. Indeed, the more knowledgeable they are, the easier it will be for all parents.

SOME OVERALL CONCLUSIONS

The two principal beneficiaries of new federal legislation are students and parents, but it will not be a cakewalk for either. Students will be expected to work harder and smarter, to satisfy higher standards and meet higher levels of achievement, to pass tests again and again, including one for graduation, to make steady and adequate yearly progress, to forego social promotion, and to attend school more days and hours and during summers. In short, the current group of students from ages three to twenty-two will encounter a more intense, tasking, and challenging educational future than any generation as a whole has ever faced before. Although it is a tight and totally inclusive system with little or no room for slack or evasion, it does allow some time for compliance. Hopefully, it provides enough time for turnaround. But unless wholesale exceptions are made, draconian sanctions will be applied to all non- or low-performing schools. In short, for many students who have just coasted along and gotten away with the minimum, their school lives will change radically.

In many ways, parents can make the difference, as in fact they often have, but now their role is officially and nationally mandated. In many cases, they have no other choice other than to become involved in, partner, and lead schools if their offspring are to benefit from and manage the tougher road of improvement. But most important is what parents do at home to implement the teacher–parent compact. That is going to be where the rubber hits the road and change occurs or does not. In other words, parents and students are more in tandem than they have ever been before; both will have to change if they are to be successful together. Schooling and mutual learning will require a closer bonding than ever before. Student success will become increasingly intertwined with parent success. They will in effect become partners or colearners. Given that shared commitment, it might be more accurate to claim that schools now and in the future enroll not just kids but families. Indeed, the name of the national law perhaps should be changed to no family left out, behind, or uninvolved.

One plea to parents: be persistent and patient with schools and educators. The culture is not used to being cooperative. It is also not used to being questioned or challenged, except by its school boards. However, now the parents' right to know essentially makes every parent a member of a larger school board. It is a whole new world of accountability for schools to accept and implement in a relatively short period of time.

By patiently and gradually negotiating new relationships and compacts with schools and teachers, parents should take the high road, where the optimum exchange and relationship can be found. Ideally, parents have to become partners with teachers just as they have to with their children. In that way parents may serve as bridges between the two. Teachers will gradually recognize that they cannot achieve the higher standards or have them last and stay in place without the input and involvement of parents. Parents in turn will become increasingly aware that the school cannot do it alone, and that without the contributions of the home their children will fall short not only of meeting higher standards, but also of achieving their full promise.

Parents thus are the key. They hold up and sustain the bridge that straddles the achievement gaps of both school and their children. Being a parent has never been more important and pivotal than now.

PRELIMINARY POSTMORTEM AND UPDATE

NCLB already is leaving its tough mark on schools across the country in the following ways:

1. Typically as much as 50 percent of the teaching staffs of all fifty states are not highly qualified. That designates teachers who do not hold a teaching credential or are insufficiently trained in their subject matter areas. Many have been terminated.
2. Between 30 and 60 percent of schools nationally have been designated as needing improvement.
3. The requirement to designate such schools has activated many parents and led them to request changes of schools. In some school districts the number of requests exceeds the number of available openings in schools making acceptable annual progress. In other words, parents are scrambling and competing with each other for a limited number of spaces.
4. Many school districts also are utilizing more data-driven report cards, which display test scores against national standards. Such report cards in effect identify not only student but also teacher performance. When coupled with announcements of certain teachers receiving incentive bonuses for their students' scores, the scramble for high-performing schools now also involves high-performance teachers. Besides intensifying the competition of parents, it may drive up the teacher salaries of outstanding teachers to new competitive levels.
5. In Massachusetts, where a graduation exam was administered, over 6,000 students failed to pass (even after five tries). Many states are postponing giving graduation exams so that they can gear up for higher passing rates. Often local community colleges are involved because admissions are usually granted before graduation.

6. Students are being left behind. In Dade County in Florida, over 4,000 third-grade students failed the reading and math state tests and will have to repeat the grade. The elimination of social promotion and NCLB mandate passing both tests. Many angry parents are claiming that NCLB should be amended to read "no child left back."

7. A major debate has emerged about whether to include special education and bilingual children in the third-grade testing mix. If the general answer is affirmative, and those students are among those left back, the net result may be a reduction of the number of special students and in bilingual education classes advocated either by school districts worried about their overall score or parents concerned about their kids having to repeat a grade.

8. Economics is contributing to the problem. Many school districts short of funds have had to cancel summer and after-school programs that might have helped to raise student scores in general or enabled many more to pass third-grade exams. Florida, under a state mandate to reduce class size, and not having sufficient funds to hire more teachers, has just reduced the number of credits required for students to graduate high school one year earlier from twenty-four to eighteen. The hope is that that will reduce the overall total number of students whose classes have to be made smaller. That reduction comes from eliminating all courses in the arts, life skills, and physical education, just as many schools have stripped the curriculum of all subjects except those being tested.

9. Alternative schooling may thrive. Because private and parochial schools are exempt from NCLB, there may be greater advocacy for vouchers (many states already offer them) to facilitate transfers to these schools. If some states or the federal government provide a tax credit for homeschooling, the alternative movement also may gain ground; but in return for economic aid there will be greater oversight.

10. Above all, parents increasingly will become both activists on behalf of better schools and advocates for their kids. If the latter prevails, as understandably it frequently does, and if it comes down to what is best for their kids, whether or not they join the

chorus blaming schools for failing their kids, they will become increasingly aggressive and resourceful. They will compete for the best schools and teachers. They will avail themselves of the subsidized tutoring provided in NCLB. They will examine their kids' school records and monitor closely the performance profiles of the schools their kids attend. In short, parent involvement will become not only an option but also a norm. Partnership will become not the exception but the rule of the way parents and schools operate together.

One final postscript about the impact of NCLB, especially the issue of students having to be left behind. Many parents may be shocked. They also may regard the impact on their kids as traumatic. But minimally two courses of action are open to parents on behalf of kids who have to repeat a grade.

First, become heavily involved in and committed to tutoring. Use established tutoring or after-school services. The tutoring provision of NCLB has been called the Sylvan amendment, because Sylvan will likely dominate the market. Parents have to become tutors, siblings have to be involved, bright teenagers should be hired, and play dates should be supplemented with study dates. Above all, be wary of your child being given a second year of exactly the same kinds of things that did not work the first time around. Examine the different approaches of Glasser and Gardner discussed in the next chapters.

Second, develop an early warning system. Catch problems before they harden into failure. Here is a sample preventative medicine checklist vigilant and proactive parents should use for their kids:

- Has low test scores and weak report cards. Hold immediate conferences with the teacher on implications and future impacts.
- Has homework problems.
- Sloppily tracks when assignments are due and test dates.
- Avoids going to school; complains of aches and pains in the morning.
- Avoids talking about school.
- Stops reading or has trouble reading.
- Complains of being bored and even unhappy in school.

- Spends most of the time watching TV or playing video games.
- Is generally listless and unmotivated.

In short, whatever problems are created by the schools, teachers, and NCLB, parents have to become assertive. There is now too much at stake, too many complex choices to make and directions to take, for parents to be anything but in charge and taking the initiative on behalf of their kids. Hopefully, this book can help by being your ally and advance guard.

2

GLASSER AND THE PSYCHOLOGY OF ACHIEVEMENT AND FAILURE*

In the introduction, I claimed that this book was not a psychological manual on child-rearing. I now have to hedge that somewhat. Clearly, emotion and intelligence impact each other. The interactive processes between home and school, between parents and teachers, between family environments and school environments regularly also involve the bridging of psychology and pedagogy. Most recently, the complex interaction between genetics (nature) and families (nurture) has been added to the mix.

Pairing the above and bridging the dynamics of each set requires in turn a fusion of Freud and Dewey, a mutual understanding of the human psyche and the nature of schools. Therapy needs to be anchored in sociology. The only psychiatrist who has moved the couch into the schools, and who in the process has made the psychology of schools into a school of psychology, is William Glasser.

To Glasser, schools are not abstract objects of study; they are where learning and behavior intersect. Glasser is directly involved in that dynamic. He has created the William Glasser Institute in Chatsworth, California, to train educators to become Quality Teachers operating Quality Schools. Conducted without fear or punishment, and without

---

*All quotations in this chapter are from William Glasser, *The Quality School: Managing Students without Coercion*, New York: Harper, 1998.

coercion, teachers and administrators of more than a dozen such schools nationally justify hearkening to his psychological analysis of schooling.

His central and most pivotal insight is that schools represent for many young children their first introduction to failure. Often that is followed by repeated failures, hastened by being dubbed so by teachers who pass such negative judgments on to other teachers. Working with "incorrigible" girls from dysfunctional families, Glasser found that even here most of their problems at home with their parents revolved around school failure.

Kids often come to school happy and open, and rapidly become serious and even grim. For the first time many encounter rules. There are so many and they are so totally prescriptive that the children themselves become obsessed by rules to the point where they even become maintainers and enforcers. Happiness is defined as obeying the rules. Then there are the tests. Do you know your letters, your address, your phone number? At home or in nursery school that was play and not such a big deal. Trial and error took kids through challenges, but now the teacher encourages obedience and performance. There are right and wrong things to do, and right and wrong answers; and they are recorded, they are known to everyone in class, and they are reported to parents. In short, Glasser claims that more often than not, children are introduced to failure in schools.

It is often persistent, sometimes lifelong. It is not unusual for adults to confess that they suffer from a block in math or English. When pressed for why and when that happened, they rapidly go back to their early grades and even can resurrect with intense emotion the name of the teacher and sometimes the specific incident that traumatized them or arrested their development. Equally as tenacious is the momentum of failure in poor and mostly urban neighborhoods. Aside from leading to later serious problems of truancy, delinquency, and criminality, Glasser estimates that 75 percent of later students experiencing school failure have not achieved a satisfactory elementary school experience. In fact, if nothing is done by the time they are ten years old, they are lost. Even suburban homes and parents may be unable to correct failure in school. Indeed, conviction of that is what led Glasser to become committed to education—to fixing the problem at its source.

What are the pernicious dynamics of failure? According to Glasser, the two basic building blocks of emotional health are caring and self-worth. Together they form identity. Love is outward directed; it involves helping others—one's classmates in this case. Ultimately such actions also build self-love and self-acceptance. Self-worth is thus initially and finally defined in interpersonal relations. However, failure destroys both. Being wounded, one withdraws. Called upon to answer questions, students retreat into the blank darkness of silence. Their task is to get through and endure things, not to enjoy them. Finding themselves devalued, they get good at devaluing themselves—better and faster than any teacher or their friends can do. In addition, there does not appear to be a second chance, because teachers pass on their lack of self-worth to other teachers. And so it goes. Indeed, when they finally do flourish later with a certain teacher, parents wish they could have that same teacher in every grade and thus ensure the continuity of success; and knowing that they can't, they brace themselves for disaster.

Glasser does not mince words: "Very few children come to school failures, none come labeled as failures; it is school and school alone that pins the label of failure on children." Glasser concludes:

> A child that has functioned satisfactorily for five years is confident that he will continue to do so in school. . . . this confidence may wane but still remain effective for about five more years. If however the child experiences failure in school from ages five to ten, by the age of ten his confidence will be shattered, his motivation will be destroyed and he will have begun to identify with failure.

To Glasser, fixing kids without fixing the schools that created the problems in the first place makes no sense. And so he launched his Quality School movement and created his own training institute for educators. That is fine for those relatively few lucky parents whose kids attended a Glasser school. But what about all the other parents? What can they do?

If they are lucky, they may find a Glasser school where they live (they are listed on his website). Failing that, parents can lean more about the corrective diagnostics and solutions Glasser advocates. Although providing a detailed summary of Glasser's key principles and practices is beyond the scope of this book and besides would be best accomplished by reading Glasser directly, what can be distilled here are a series of warning signs:

1. Any signs of failure.
2. Early signs of giving up or surrender.
3. Any reluctance to go to school.
4. Avoidance at home of anything associated with schools.
5. Picking friends who are poor school performers.
6. Mood changes.
7. Preference for isolation rather than play.
8. Excessive TV watching, video game playing, or computer use.
9. Sudden bursts of anger or impatience.
10. Loss of appetite.

Although finding such behaviors may also be related to other matters at home, what correctives can generally be employed by parents?

1. Have rapid, frequent, and detailed conversations with teachers.
2. If there appears after repeated consultation to be a personality or other conflict between the teacher and student, don't wait too long. Make an appointment with the guidance counselor to address change of teachers. Save the principal as a court of last resort. In many school districts parents have the right, seldom publicized, to request change of teachers.
3. Generally monitor the feedback from other parents about the teachers their kids have, especially at the next grade level. Identify the best matches available.
4. Request that the teacher pinpoint specific problem areas. Don't accept generalized observations. If the student is scheduled to be taken out of class for special Title I help, move rapidly to prevent that decision from being entered into his or her school record.
5. Create an alternative to the school at home—a partial home-school—with tutors: parents, siblings, older kids, professional tutors if you can afford to hire them.
6. The parents of some homeschooled kids schedule play and study dates. They combine socialization with skills acquisition in a relaxed environment.

7. Consider using learning centers, but if costs and time involved are nearly equal, stay with individual tutors. Their loyalty is to the student, not the center's bottom line.

8. Benchmark where the student was when the tutoring started. Check with the teacher periodically as to what changes he or she has perceived. Make sure those changes are noted in writing and on report cards.

9. Share improvements with the guidance counselor and if appropriate with the principal.

10. Be patient. Operate on the leapfrog expectation; while catching up, try to get ahead.

To some extent, the national approach of NCLB and Glasser's generic analysis both underscore school failure as a national problem. Certainly, the emphasis of NCLB especially in urban areas finds concurrence in Glasser's conclusion: "Although educational failure is widespread in all communities, it exists in epidemic proportions in the poor neighborhoods of cities. For all practical purposes education in the central city is itself a failure." But parents and students in other environments are not immune from the almost congenital, structural, and systemic role of schools to be places of failure.

Glasser's solution is to change the schools. Parents have two options: they can support school reform à la Glasser, or they can provide home and familial alternatives. Returning happier students with greater self-worth to the school not only obviously improves the lot of your kids, but also offers a contrast to what may be going on there. If enough parents do that, then the exception may become the new norm, and more schools happily may become more Glasser-like. But if change does not occur, parents have to take charge, as will be detailed in the next chapter.

3

CREATING QUALITY HOMES AND PARENTS

Dr. William Glasser, applying his psychiatric skills to education, has pioneered a movement to create Quality Schools and Quality Teachers across the U.S. Toward that end, he has established the William Glasser Institute in Chatsworth, California, written books, and developed an elaborate network of schools and trainers. The training time and process are extensive and complex for two reasons.

First, Glasser is convinced that nothing less than a complete overhaul of the basic school culture can prepare the groundwork for building quality schools and teachers. History and habit create formidable obstacles to change. Second, Glasser also believes that the process must be totally inclusive. It must involve all teachers, staff, and administrators for the school as whole to move forward as an intact, coherent, and coordinated force. Such inclusiveness takes time—usually three to five years.

Although throughout the training process parents are involved, the extent and nature of their participation tends to be occasional, partial, and generally indirect. Thus, parents may be invited to observe, but generally not speak, at demonstrations of the dynamics of class discussions. Typically they are neither part of instructional training nor of special training sessions designed or held for parents. On the one hand, that is understandable; the focus has to be on schools and teachers. On the other hand, parents are a critical reinforcing force; indeed, how critical they are appears from Glasser's own analysis.

Glasser invests home and family with two pivotal roles. The first occurs before school starts. The formative years from birth to nursery school or kindergarten lay the foundations for later happiness and student success, yet the parents are not provided with Glassers's proactive guidelines for raising infants and toddlers. The second matter is perhaps more critical. Glasser claims that if kids encounter failure, it occurs in schools; and sadly such failure tends to last, even lifelong. Glasser, for example, found that the problems of teenage delinquents ultimately had roots in school failure. Moreover, once a kid fails, the system almost maliciously perpetuates and passes on that failure to those next in line to the point where it becomes a self-fulfilling prophecy, fixed and permanent in the minds and behaviors of subsequent teachers. The idea of a new grade and teacher as a blank slate is an illusion.

Glasser notes that often the antidote and corrective to school failure is supplied by the home and parents. However, the telltale signs of or early warning system for such failure are not described symptomatically to and for parents to detect and respond to in advance, nor are the specific corrective antidotes provided.

The one happy exception is his new book on helping parents talk to teenagers, but that is rightly more oriented to mental health than to school success (although clearly they are ultimately one). In addition, because it focuses on the later years, parents again are not provided with the earlier interventions and options for action that might have prevented or altered the angry dynamics of parent-teenager exchanges. In short, there is a need to translate quality schools and teachers into quality homes and parents. At least that way if neither the school nor the teachers subscribe to quality, parents can fill the gap and their offspring may have more of a fighting chance. Indeed, parents' final trump card may be to elect homeschooling.

The starting point of carryover then is to identify the key ingredients and processes of Glasser's Quality Schools. The end point is to translate and apply those elements so as to define Quality Homes. The goal is to create a mirror match, an alignment of goals and roles that will enable quality homes and parents to reinforce quality schools and teachers. Sadly, if such coincidence is lacking, parents at least can take up the slack and pursue an alternative and independent course to ensure the mental well-being and learning success of their offspring.

There are five basic components of the Glasser model:

1. Quality.
2. Driving needs.
3. Choice instead of coercion.
4. Conversational relationships.
5. Happiness.

What ties together all five goals is that they are all process-driven; require constant action and intervention; are invariably affectionate and patient; never steal decisions from those who have to live them; and always require parents or teachers to be involved in mutual growth partnerships with their students and offspring. In short, a Quality School or Home is not the result of tweaking and revising existing situations or operations. Rather each requires a totally new system in its own right.

I. QUALITY

What is it? To understand quality requires examining why Glasser uses the term in the first place. Three factors are involved. The first is that Glasser introduces quality because he claims typically it is not routinely present in schools. What passes for quality is competence; but quality is always beyond competence, although students routinely are seduced to settle for competence because it is presented as equal to and granted an A grade.

When Glasser interviewed outstanding students, they regularly confessed that what schools accepted as their best work was not the best they could do—it was not quality. Quality, then, always involves a stretch beyond competence. It always requires the next step or two not taken. It is not unlike Robert Frost's classic poem, "The Road Not Taken," in which two roads diverged in the wood and the speaker selected the one less traveled by, which "has made all the difference."

Second, quality is not elitist. It is not reserved for only the brightest students; rather, it is available to all. In fact, it is the great leveler; it optimizes access. No student is excluded, because quality is not so much a specific end point as an end process. The final arrival point, as well as how long it may take, may vary with each student. But the critical focus is that that final destination always involves taking the next step or the road less traveled by. Quality thus pushes competence to excellence. Although such excellence is individual, the extra step always earns everyone who takes it the A grade. The mark of excellence is thus to be found in the extra effort, in the fidelity to constant improvement. It is thus not unlike the frequent practice in math of giving extensive credit for the right method even though the answer may be incorrect.

Third, quality defines not just work but interpersonal relationships; or rather, sustaining quality relationships requires work. Here, too, what rules and defines the process is taking the next step, making the extra effort, going the extra mile; moving the process beyond merely being a competent teacher or parent into modeling quality relationships.

Glasser provides a five-step process to structure the pursuit of quality. It is summed up by the acronym, SESIR:

SHOW: Present what has been done and/or described in both work and interpersonal relationships.

EXPLAIN: Examine how such work and/or relationships came about and what the student did to bring that achievement or relationship to this point.

SELF-REVIEW: Evaluate what has been done to see how good it is and to consider what can be further done to improve it.

IMPROVEMENT: Set about developing and implementing an improvement plan.

REPETITION: Improvement is not one but many steps. It is continuous.

Help can be sought along the way at any stage. The process continues until the point is reached when further attempts at improvement are not worth the effort. That last revision designates quality for that person at that time and earns an A. In other words, the top grade is given whenever a student has in effect exceeded himself and gone beyond the minimum to the maximum.

This five-step process is what Glasser believes should be the way all teachers should teach and evaluate all students at all grade levels from kindergarten to twelfth grade. Such a recurrent and across-the-board process from the outset introduces and anchors quality in the schools as a common expectation of all. Carried over into the home, SESIR can enable families constantly to review, restart, and improve their relationships with each other. They can break free of settling for low-level grunts as family conversations, or worse, bitter acrimony and counteraccusations of blame. Above all, quality would rule both school and the home, and the quality relationships of each area would be the avenue to the other.

Two dynamics underpin and provide power to SESIR. The first is that it shifts the initiative from teacher to student, from parent to kid, and with that comes the confidence that such self-reliance is both deserved and resourceful. In other words, improvement always belongs to the one doing the improving. Taking the next step is a choice made; and taking the one step after that and even after that is owned by the one undertaking the improvements. The entire process is thus a form of progressive empowerment. Because it is ongoing and continuous throughout all the grades and all the years of growing up in the family, it builds from strength to strength and success to success.

Equally as important, the focus on improvement constantly taps and draws on inner resources for growth and change. It signals that whatever is done is never a final product but can be improved. It requires students and kids to step back and be reflective—to see their work and themselves as objects of a process that, far from being finished, is incomplete and can be made better. Although help can be given, especially when kids insist that nothing more can be done, once they are unstuck and restarted, perhaps in a new direction or with a different frame of mind, the final achievement must remain theirs. Moreover, that experience of overcoming obstacles strengthens their resolve for the next time and the task of converting competence to excellence. Above all, we come to know what quality is, to associate it with our own performance goals, and to feel good about our work and relationships.

2. NEEDS

According to Glasser, we are need-satisfying creatures driven by five needs:

- Security and caring.
- Love and friendship.
- The power of feeling important, respected, and central.
- Fun or enjoyment, laughter, and happiness.
- The freedom to be increasingly independent.

Basic security is provided by caring parents who help teach survival skills. Teachers have to recreate in their classrooms that same security to support successful survival. But too often caring and coaching are turned into rules and punishments.

The two basic sources of love are parents and friends. In the early grades teachers are in loco parentis, but all too often the affection is conditional or withheld as punishment. Unlike teachers or parents, friends never do that. That is in fact what makes them friends and what establishes the hierarchy of quality relationships.

Glasser calls self-worth power because that is what infants and toddlers discover with their cries and coos as they grow up. The child soon learns that such power is in the hands of others to bestow or to withhold. His image of self-worth is thus a contingent process. Although it is earned by what he does, control over how he is valued is vested in outside hands. Thus, self-esteem is constantly and literally a give-and-take process, a sometimes endless political negotiation. Failure damages the self, makes it feel inferior or inadequate. Sadly, it occurs in schools, especially early on. Adults who later confess to having a block to English or math usually can trace it back to a negative experience with a first- or second-grade teacher. Given such frequency and how critical the early grades are to launching students on the paths to success or failure, only the best teachers should be employed to teach the early grades, just as in enlightened colleges only the best teachers are assigned to teach freshmen.

Fun is profound. It is at the heart of all achievement. For a child, play and learning are one and the same. Fun makes learning congenial; it is a friendly, not an intimidating, process. Unfortunately, teachers early on are often grim and equate fun with childish and nonserious behavior. Learning is made into work, which is tough and has to be mastered. Play takes place outside on the playground, not in the classroom. That is how play begins to acquire a bad, almost puritanical, reputation, and is disassociated early on from learning. Schoolwork then becomes serious business; it is done by children who, as the teachers remind them, are adults-in-training. Fun comes back into their lives through extracurricular activities or sports, and hopefully at home and with their friends. Ironically, later in life many successful adults confess that the reason they are successful is that their work is like play. Frost's object in life was to make his work play and his play work. That motto should be posted in every classroom and home.

Finally, happiness, according to Glasser, is so important that it determines everything: success in school, contentment at home, and above all mental health. In fact, instead of describing people as suffering from mental illness or disease, Glasser suggests they should simply be described as unhappy. And most unhappiness does not require mind-numbing and potentially addictive psychotropic drugs, but counseling as to how happiness can be restored. Like SESIR, the key to the process of regaining happiness employs self-improvement and choice.

3. CHOICE THEORY AS THERAPY

The subtitle of Glasser's book on Quality Schools is "Managing Students without Coercion." Glasser rightly claims that the teachers we remember with affection and admiration never had class management problems, and if they did they did not solve it by strongly imposing their authority. In other words, good teachers (and good parents) are not bosses but coaches. They do not order kids around, hide behind rules, or require obedience. Instead, their favorite method of instruction is inquiry. That requires teachers and parents to invest students or offspring with power—the third need to feel important and to enjoy self-worth and self-respect. Discourse requires not only answering questions but also making choices.

Teachers and parents have to step back from running things to create the space where students and kids can think their way through to action and decision. If we are what we choose, then choice, not prescription, should start early on. Glasser demonstrates how, through asking seminal questions as part of class discussions, students can begin to think their way through problems, and begin to comprehend that a range of choices, many of which they never considered before, are now available to them.

Discussions about what makes a good student a good student, about cheating on tests, about telling lies, about bullying, and so on, deliver the reality of school behaviors into the realm of thought, feeling, and action. Students find that their ideas and how they feel about them are important—they are data; they have substance. Wisdom is not always the monopoly of adults. Kids can solve problems; they can make decisions; in short, they can choose a course of action.

Power comes from empowerment. But the key is for teachers and parents to stop being bosses of behavior and instead become leaders of choice. For that to happen, those in charge have to surrender control and coercion, their favorite weapons of authority, for inquiry and persuasion, the facilitators of self-analysis and change. They have to move from the direct to the indirect, from herding students into narrow confines to opening up wide spaces, and finally from coercion to choice.

Although often more emotionally charged, such changes in focus may be more easily put in place in the home than in the school. Only parental turnaround is required in the home, whereas in the school it has to involve all the teachers, all the staff, and all the supervisors—in short, the whole system of rules and regulations, which may have hardened into the prevailing highly directive culture. Without choice the school is basically a benevolent dictatorship and thus can never serve as model of democracy and citizenry. And then we wonder why when students grow up they fail to vote.

4. CONVERSATIONAL RELATIONSHIPS

The common complaint of both teachers and parents (often without knowing what they share) is that students do not talk. Teachers find students silent and even sullen in class. The back rows are filled with mutes who do not so much attend as endure school. If they had the option they would redesign all classrooms to resemble the pie shape of a few seats in the front and many in the back. The goodie-goodies would sit up front and the cool cats in the back.

Parents frequently complain that their kids, as they grow older, talk less and less at home or that their conversations have become an ugly series of angry exchanges or grunts. Routinely, blame and accusation escalate into the increasing defiance of kids and the ultimatums of parents. It is exhausting and exasperating, and more often than not concludes with the final acceptance on both sides of mutual failure. Like the students in class, they endure home until they can reach the point of liberation.

According to Glasser the challenge in school requires addressing relevance; in the home, the need for relationships. In both instances, the pivotal point is improvement or attitudinal change born of self-reflection. In school, teachers must be willing to explore, and wherever possible demonstrate, the relevance of what is being studied. They should not take the form of a series of pronouncements from up high: "History has been studied since the ancients and is revered and valued by intelligent people throughout time." Aside from designating students who may devalue history as unintelligent, such teachers sidestep the issue of relevance and lose the opportunity of really inviting students to go inside the subject and discovering its strength and difference. In short, the task of defining the relevance of history has to be made a significant dimension of the history course itself; and students have to be given the opportunity of regularly defining its value as a subject.

Similarly, at home and generally following the steps of SESIR, the dynamics of improvement can be introduced. The first step is to call for a truce. Second, time has to be set aside for everyone involved to sit down and identify impasses. Third, the gripes and arguments on both sides have to be aired, restated, and summed up. Fourth, ask everyone individually where they want and how they wish things to be, and examine what stands in the way of getting there. Fifth, as starters suggest improvements and changes on everyone's part to become unstuck; and if those take hold, then maybe other ones can be added. In short, conversation becomes relationships, or rather the way relationships improve.

5. HAPPINESS

Happiness is such a basic driving force to Glasser that in his most recent book he advocates replacing the notion of mental health with happiness and of mental disease with unhappiness. Happiness is the culminating embodiment of all the other four components. It engages the quality of life, satisfies the driving needs, is basically chosen, not coerced, and sustains itself with constant conversational relationships. Above all, happiness is subject to continuous improvement; it is the emotional equivalent of lifelong learning.

What this also means is that both teachers and parents themselves not only have to value and model happiness, but also make it a key goal of school and home. This is not to take the form of busywork or under-served praise or cheerleading in school or lavishing kids with material things at home. Rather, it is evidenced by a general air of contentment, by an openness to new ideas and opportunities, and above all by taking delight in play and friendships. Above all, happiness is always chosen. It is not granted as a birthright. It is not guaranteed to last. It has to be cre-ated and claimed anew every day. It is the mental health one grants one-self, often with the help of caring teachers and parents.

Happy students are always better students. They pursue quality be-cause happiness is based on improvement. Happy offspring are always better members of families. They pursue quality familial relationships because they have something critical to contribute to quality homes. The role of teachers and parents is to detect and address signs of un-happiness. SERIR has to be invoked, except in this case feelings become the objects of the process seeking improvement. Required by and in-sisted upon initially by teachers and parents, the five-step process grad-ually becomes internalized and habitual.

In the best of all possible worlds, school and home would match and each in its own way would pursue the goals of quality; and ultimately happiness and quality would become the common definition of each other. However, if quality schools and teachers are not available, by ap-plying Glasser's principles parents at least can shape quality homes, sus-tain conversations of choice, and embrace happiness as a familial goal. Having Glasser as a mentor to parents and a catalyst of family conversa-tions provides a natural extension of what he has similarly offered to teachers and schools. In the event that homeschooling is chosen, then everything becomes one: quality parents become quality teachers and quality homes become quality schools.

4

THE DIFFERENCE PARENTS CAN MAKE: WHAT THE RESEARCH SHOWS

We should start with the obvious, which is often overlooked. Here is what parents minimally contribute to student success. They ensure that their kids show up on time, washed, fed (carrying snacks or lunches), and dressed appropriately.

The first item should not be minimized. According to the Department of Justice, 81 percent of all those in jail began as truants. The figure jumps to 95 percent for juvenile offenders. Having taken care of the basics, parents hopefully equip their children with:

- Tools (pencils, pens, paper)
- Schoolbooks
- Homework completed
- Curiosity
- Happiness

The way parents themselves get up and get ready, have breakfast, and go off to work or do whatever they do, models behavior for their children. If they hate their job, moan and groan about what they have to face that day, are disorganized or forgetful about family matters or arrangements, and bolt out of the door angry or martyred, that may impact how their children go off to their day. The way home and family are managed determines how school and sibling relationships are maintained and negotiated. The key question then for parents to ask is: does the way we start our day together as a family set up our kids for success or failure in school? Morning and night times—the way we begin and the way we end the day—are the optimum points for parents and families.

What else does the research show about the impact of parents on kids and school? Here are some of the findings:

PARENTAL IMPACT

1. Children whose parents help them at home and stay in touch with the school score higher than children of similar aptitude and family background whose parents are not involved.
2. Programs designed with strong parent involvement produce students and schools that perform better than those with little or no involvement.
3. Schools that relate to their communities have student bodies that outperform other schools.
4. Schools where children are failing improve dramatically when parents are called in to help.
5. Parental involvement in school raises the standards of home life.
6. Schools report that parent involvement programs prove to be one of the most cost-effective ways of increasing student achievement.
7. More involved parents become more effective people in general, often changing the way they do everything, including their jobs.
8. Learning more about their rights as parents often leads them to greater community involvement.

THE STUDENT SUCCESS FACTORS

The research also identifies the critical success factors. They are five in number:

- Time on task
- High expectations

- Parental involvement
- Safety
- School leadership

Being third on the list is obviously important, especially because parental involvement is the only factor outside of school. Yet when one considers that time on task, high expectations, and safety are also inextricable parts of many home environments, parental involvement suddenly ranks higher than or as high as the first two. Indeed, when most of the success factors are subsumed under parent involvement, what emerge are basically only two kinds of leadership on behalf of student success: school leadership and home leadership.

Zeroing in closer, how important is home environment to student success? For decades, the conventional wisdom was that success was driven exclusively by SES—socioeconomic status. The higher the levels of educational and social standing, the more money one earned, the more advanced one's job and position was, and so on, the more likely offspring of such parents would be successful in school. In general, those predictors held up except for one stubborn difference: they could not account for kids from poor-SES homes achieving significant academic success. This was a particularly disturbing and important anomaly for a country that regularly acculturates new waves of immigrants.

Later research sought to confront the problem directly. Instead of using SES as a gross and intact indicator of success, it was broken down into four subfactors: income, parental education, parental occupation, and home atmosphere. Remarkably, home atmosphere turned out to bear the strongest relationship to student achievement. For the first time researchers had found the basis for understanding how students with low SES but a positive home environment could do so well in school. In short, nurture triumphed over nature for a change. Equally as important, that research opened up the broader questions of what shapes a good home environment and what parenting styles work best.

HOME ENVIRONMENTS

The homes that contributed most to student success feature communication, supervision, and aspiration.

Communication

Supportive parents value conversation. The home is generally not a silent place or filled only with the sound of the airwaves. The TV does not stay on all the time. Parents always find the time and the place to discuss school, friends, activities, clothes, movies. They often insist on common meal times. Whenever possible breakfast is a daily focus (except on weekends); no one leaves without breakfast. If that meal won't work because kids have to leave at different times, dinner assumes the position of being a command performance. Even with crazy schedules there have to be at least one or two nights a week that are absolutely and officially designated as family meal time.

Families create their own traditions and cultures. Kids planning the menu and cooking once a month becomes a family ritual. Going to a pizza parlor after school events is another. But eating and talking together are important. There are no exceptions—both mothers and fathers have to be there and have to practice what they teach. They regularly need to talk to each other and to place a high value in the family on interpersonal relationships through conversations.

Parents should always be genuinely curious about and interested in their kids—in what they are learning and studying. Some parents use the "one big idea" icebreaker: "What is the one big idea you discovered today in school that you did not know yesterday?" Parents also often weave into such discussions materials and items from books, articles, or the newspaper they have read. At the right time and place they might raise, for example, Glasser's notion of school and failure or whether teachers talk openly and knowledgeably about NCLB. Parents have to become particularly adept at detecting avoidance or questioning silence; there may be something deeper going on. So they gently probe. They ask questions. They may develop over time a checklist. If nothing is elicited except impatience, they may have to wait. Having planted the seed, time needs to be given for it to grow. If kids are upset, they may well come and talk to you later—you just have to be patient.

Effective two-way communication does not come easy; it involves hard work and ingenuity. It is never achieved once and for all time. It also may have to change over time as your kids grow up. Like love it has to kept up to date. You lose what you don't use; it has to be renewed and kept alive every day. It must not be allowed to be taken for granted or made into a mechanical ritual, and it has to be two-way. Monologue is not dialogue. Avoid the threatening and accusing finger of indignant self-righteousness. Communication is never automatic or easy, which is why many parents give up and settle into small talk or silence; it constantly requires parental availability. Parents first always have to be there, open and ready to put aside whatever they are doing to make room and time for whatever their kids want to talk about.

Supervision

A home should be safe and secure, it should be open and friendly, and it should always be busy, even if the activities are silent ones. But homes require structure. They require boundaries of time and place; they function within limits. That is what Moms and Dads do. That is what parents do when they do not try to become pals or friends to their kids. Kids have their own peers. They want their parents to remain parents, and that means structure.

Supervision need not be harsh or incessantly invasive, but it should involve the watchful eye that misses nothing. It should involve constant monitoring. Parents should always know where their kids are, what they are doing, and with whom. In turn their kids should know that drill, and that hiding such information is not an option. Parents need to know when kids leave for school and when they are due to return, where they are going ("Just out" is not an acceptable destination) with friends ("The guys" does not work either), and above all when they must be back ("Call if it is more than 15 minutes later").

One of the most difficult problems parents face with supervision occurs when their family culture and parental structure are at odds with those of their friends. For some perverse reason the more permissive arrangement is always thrown up in the face of the more structured parents. Swinging and square parents are like East and West; they do not meet. But such contrasts should not be threatening or lead to harsh absolutes or above all to criticism of a different family style. Parents should just quietly but firmly hold their ground, remain steady, and stay the course. In the long run consistency may match conversation in value and durability.

Monitoring also requires how much time kids study and spend on their homework and preparing for tests (more about this important activity later in the book); how much reading they do in their free time; and above all how much time they spend on the phone, watch TV, or play video games. The new culprit is the Internet, which has eclipsed TV in terms of attention and which also carries the additional worrisome dimension of blocking porn and unsolicited proposals. To be sure, it also has provided electronic communication that enormously supports and reinforces the supervisory role of parents in some school districts. Although that has engendered some mixed reactions of Big Brother, especially and understandably from kids, it is part of the new future of home and schools and of their more interactive relationships. In any case, the problem of supervision will remain critical because studies show that there is a negative correlation between watching TV excessively and student achievement.

Aspiration

Once again parents set the standard. When they themselves show regular signs of self-improvement and lifelong education, when for example they read instead of watching TV, attend lectures or cultural events, plan trips or vacations which are both fun and informative, they are essentially practicing the art of aspiration. It is obviously OK to go to Disney, but include Epcot and swimming with dolphins.

Specifically, parents also have to communicate the academic goals of finishing high school, attending college, going to graduate or professional schools, avoiding drugs and alcohol, and above all not allowing gender or racial stereotypes to force girls to be nurses when they have the ability to be doctors.

Often here parental histories come into play, especially those stirred by regret or triumph. There is the father who works in a factory warning his sons that if he ever learns that any of them has taken a factory job, even if it is only for the summer, he will break both their legs and arms. It would make his life a failure and a mockery. Or the mother who relates how she was pressured into marrying too early or not going to college by her mother who told her: "Smart men don't marry smart women." Families just getting by financially will often stress how costly college is and how it further takes away time from earning income and contributing to the family. One of the recurrent tales, especially in certain cultures, is that of young men and women sacrificing their future careers to help the family out. And so it goes.

There is no hard-and-fast rule. Personal parental histories are often so powerful and urgent that they cannot be suppressed. But told again and again they lose the power of application, and they become associated with a would-a, should-a, could-a attitude that kids ultimately reject. A better version is exemplified when a parent tries to do something about remedying that decision or at least accepting it. The worst thing is to try to live your unlived life through that of your kids. We also have learned that for every kid who wants to follow in his or her father's or mother's footsteps there is one who is determined not to.

The favorite, and in some families the obsessive, topic of what careers their offspring will aspire to and finally choose is more complicated and complex than ever before. First, the subject is surfacing earlier. School choice has compelled many families to be involved in more school planning sooner than they thought. Second, new jobs never heard of are surfacing. One of their kids interested in computer science casually indicates at the dinner table that he plans to become a video game designer. All the other kids say "Cool!" while the parents sit dumbfounded. Worse, parents exhibit knee-jerk negative reactions of rejection instead of asking what that is and what does it involve. Third, in many families where the kids have allowances and sometimes their own credit cards, parental arguments of picking a career that offers security instead of chancy growth often fall on deaf ears. Besides, the future of the economy and of jobs in general is a mystery even to the experts. The wisest course is to keep the conversation of aspiration and choice open and unfinished and resist all efforts to resolve it prematurely or to cut off later positioning. Structure can be open-ended and still be structure.

But the home is not an island unto itself. Good communication, supervision, and aspiration in the home are shaped in turn by the relationships between the school and the home, and between educators and parents, and they have not always been, nor are they now, happy.

HOME AND SCHOOL

The basic problem historically is that schools not only have taken parents for granted, but have also limited their roles and contributions. Typically teachers have defined parental roles in negative terms. Parents can raise money but teachers alone decide what it can be used for. They can discuss textbooks, but teachers choose them. They can discuss the curriculum and even homework, but again teachers make the final decisions. It is not any different with administrators who hide behind confidentiality, board decisions, and public policy to preclude discussion or action.

However, all that is changing. It is a new day and future for parents for two basic reasons. First, the current generation of parents is too well educated, empowered, assertive, and organized to be cowed. They know their rights. Often, they are more aware of the provisions of NCLB than the teachers or administrators are, invoke the Freedom of Information Act, and will take districts or boards to court. Second, both educators and parents read the same research. Both know how important the home is and how parental involvement and support can make the difference as to whether their students, school, and district achieve their mandated goals or suffer the consequences. In short, whether through desperation or enlightenment or a mixture of the two rules, teachers and parents are now joined at the hip. This new relationship now has affected and even changed their three shared activities: communication, participation, and governance.

Communication between School and Home

The two standard and time-honored exchanges between teacher and parents occur at open school night at the beginning of the school year and parent–teacher conferences. The first is often frustrating. Aside from meeting and sizing up their kid's new teacher, parents are told that this is not the time for individual conferences (which is all that parents are really interested in in the first place and will use every occasion to slip in). Rather it is a time to understand the plan and goals for the year in that class or subject matter. It is often presented in such a cut-and-dry, mechanical way that it is both boring and uninformative; and parents are fearful that it will impact their kids the same way. Hardly ever is it explained in terms of the dynamics of student learning, let alone parent follow-up, or a sample segment demonstrated as an actual lesson. In short, many parents find that opening night to be a token show of communication, but essentially a waste of time; and if the school wants to build a lasting and more meaningful relationship with parents, they should never waste the valuable and limited time of parents.

The parent–teacher conference is often not more satisfying. First, it is scheduled usually only after or before school. Many mothers work or have little ones at home who cannot be left alone. Fathers usually cannot come. Second, the agenda is not known. Even when report cards are to be discussed, the teacher, not the parent, is fortified with all the information, test scores, and homework papers. Parents afterwards wished they had made copies of their kid's homework and had come equipped with their own folder of supportive materials. In other words, the conferencing is usually one-sided. The teacher talks and the parent listens. Third, parents often leave with a sense of confusion and disparity. They do not fully recognize the image of their kid that has just been portrayed. They believe they know their kids, but not what has been shown. They may begin to doubt their own knowledge. On the defensive, they also may begin to accept the teacher's portrait and react with greater suspicion or even mistrust of their instincts or what their kids say to them. Meanwhile, the teacher, who may be a parent herself, is oblivious of the impact she has had. Happily, much of this seems to be changing; and parents more than educators are initiating the changes.

Changing Communication Patterns

The first matter to be changed is scheduling of home and school events. Recently, a new principal in western Massachusetts related an interesting story. She was upset to learn that less than 50 percent of parents showed up for open school night and only slightly more for parent–teacher conferences. The conclusion of the teachers was that parents just don't care; they are not that interested in the school or their kids' progress. The superintendent was reluctant to believe that, and so he constructed a survey and sent it to all parents.

The results were surprising. Over 80 percent were two-income families. Even in single-wage-earner families, the breadwinner has taken another job, often in the evenings or on weekends, to make ends meet. Over 40 percent still had preschoolers or little ones at home and could not get or afford to get babysitters so that they could come to school. The favorite—in some cases the only—day both parents were free to come to school was Saturday morning; and then hopefully babysitting would be provided.

Three weeks later, open school and parent–teacher meetings were scheduled on Saturday morning. Babysitters were provided. The superintendent paid for coffee and doughnuts. The attendance was nearly perfect. Unexpectedly, many grandparents living with their kids—in a few instances raising their grandkids—showed up and helped with the babysitting or sat in on the conferences. The superintendent leaned over and whispered to her assistant, "Make a note to develop a special program for grandparents raising grandkids."

It is amazing how much can be learned when assumptions can be put aside and simple questions asked. It is equally surprising, when something like parental involvement becomes a priority, how resourceful and even creative schools can become. In fact, in the last few years schools have dramatically changed the ways they communicate with parents. In addition to more flexible scheduling, it has involved:

- Home telephone calls in the evenings
- Home visits
- Student-led parent–teacher conferences
- 360-degree student profiles
- Electronic links between school and home

Although the last three will require greater elaboration and discussion later, what these signal is a rapid and significant change in the communication relationships between teachers and parents. Not surprisingly, that also has carried over to the related areas of participation and governance.

Participation

Current and evolving relationships go way beyond bake sales, although fund-raising has become more important to financially strapped schools. Parents have formed financial foundations to raise money for computers, professional development workshops, teacher attendance at state and national conferences, and so on. In a small town in Oregon, a budget shortfall led to the termination of an excellent teacher. Parents raised the equivalent of her salary and benefits and saved her job. In short, parents are now making a financial difference as well.

But participation has gone further. Many parents function as teacher's aides, tutors, and guest lecturers. Teachers welcome their added expertise as well as the greater capacity of their classroom to offer differentiated and individualized instruction. Above all, when teachers can find the time, they are developing follow-up lesson plans adjusted for each child to share with and be implemented by parents at home. So conceived and structured, homework becomes not separate or unrelated but an integrated and continuous part of schooling, with the teacher and parent working cooperatively in tandem with each other. However, for that to happen and to happen effectively, the priority of parental involvement and participation must alter the basic school schedule as well (as will be noted later). What is clear is that just as communication has changed, so has participation; and we have not seen the full extent of both, partly because of what is happening and will continue to happen in the area of governance.

Governance

Direct political access to schools by parents historically has been driven by two forces: their rights as taxpayers and voters on school referenda; and the access mandated by or provided for by public legislation. Their direct participation in school governance emerged in the 1960s and 1970s with the addition to Title I reauthorization acts to create Parent Advisory Councils or PACs. Many functioned separately as individual councils taking on or usurping the prerogative of elected school boards. Some in effect became the school board. A number were co-opted and became part of new site-based management teams advising principals on policy issues. Although later legislation removed the requirement of every school district requiring a PAC (many had become incredibly contentious and disruptive), a residual effect remained. Parents still serve on many site-based teams and are regularly invited to be part of search committees seeking new teachers, principals, and superintendents.

The major fear of educators is that parents will run the schools. Aside from the prospect that given the way schools are currently managed, they probably could not do any worse and might even do better, that is not the kind of governance parents seek. An extensive survey in six states by Stallworth and Williams in 1982 revealed that parents are not interested in running or micromanaging schools. However, they are interested and are determined to know how the overall management of schools impacts directly on their kids, and until schools and educators recognize that central fact and find the ways to explain that critical relationship, the issue of parental governance will not go away.

PARENTAL STYLES

There is one final issue as to what the research shows. Parents tend to exhibit or practice three different parental styles: authoritarian, permissive, and persuasive. The research favors the last and in fact shows that the first two bear little or no relationship to lasting student achievement. Why?

The authoritarian style employs the carrot-and-stick approach of military discipline. Alternately using bribery or fear, attraction and avoidance, it assumes that motivation can be imposed from without, but generally it either does not work or take hold. Besides, it requires constant external application of the cookie or the two-by-four. The fact is motivation cannot be created. It is only an internal affair. Emerging from within, motivation can be encouraged and directed. But the old saw is still true: you can lead a horse to water but you can't make him drink. He has to be thirsty, and he has to trust that the water is drinkable.

The problem with the authoritarian style is that it often forecloses discussion and limits further options. It frequently leads to ultimatums, which are later regretted, but it is often too late; the damage has been done. Such absolute decisions are frequently not shared or even discussed but are pushed or promulgated by one parent, often in the heat of the moment, and thus drive a wedge between the two. Like adults, children do not like to be bullied and backed into a corner. Everyone wants choices. Everyone wants a say in decisions that affect them. Ironically, many parents who have been involved in empowered teams at work and have learned how critical it is to secure and negotiate consensus do not carry their work experience over to their homes and families.

Many authoritarian parents justify that stance by invoking the excesses of the permissive style. They cite chapter and verse of kids on drugs or teenage pregnancies as the inevitable results of laxity. Their kids listen to such a litany and roll their eyes in disbelief. They even may make matters worse unintentionally by defending their friends, only to find an authoritarian parent concluding that they are defending the behavior as well. It is a no-win escalating situation.

The problem with the permissive style is that kids need structure. They do not know what to do with their increasing energy. Boundaries need to be drawn within which they can function and be content. As they grow older and want more space and freedom, the boundaries are not thrown out altogether but redrawn and renegotiated. One cannot play tennis with the net down.

It has been found that persuasion works best in part because it combines and integrates the other two major components of communication and supervision. It also is nonpunitive and patient and routinely empowers kids with choices and decisions that they have to live with and up to. It shifts the initiative of discussion and recommendation (not the final decision) increasingly to them. They have their say and so do you, but you decide the final direction to be taken. Care has to be taken that choices are not lubricated or programmed by tangible rewards or incentives. That may convey not only a value system that is questionable, but also result in parents having to up the ante of the bribe next time. The best reward still is cementing and celebrating parental relationships with their kids, whether it take the form of a pizza party or renting a video tape and making popcorn.

The centrality of the family is the core relationship, especially for single-parent families. That offers the key to everything: emotional health, role modeling, caring relationships, self-worth, durable identities, and aspiration and student achievement. To give the persuasive style a fighting chance of steering a middle path between the authoritarian and permissive styles, parents have to forge a compact with each other which minimally includes the following:

- Issue no ultimatums, ever.
- Make no unilateral decisions.
- There have to be two yes's or two no's for a decision.
- A split decision is not a decision.
- Try not to fight or criticize each other in front of the kids.

- If you must argue, wait until the kids are asleep, and go off for a walk or rent a motel room.
- Never go to bed angry with each other.
- Mothers and fathers need to remain husbands and wives to each other. Such open physical affection is the best form of sex education.
- Begin to carve out, anticipate, and prepare your own future lives as individuals and with each other. . . . Develop future plans.
- Kids grow up and ultimately leave; and you still have lives to lead and grandchildren perhaps to welcome into the world of choices. Before that happens and while you are still raising your kids, become aware of the changing school roles of parents and the future of education. The two are increasingly on a converging course and you don't want your kids to get crushed between them.

Part 2

CHANGING CHANGE

Things are not the way they used to be. This is especially true of education and today's kids, and ultimately for the kind of parent you may have to be.

Parents today have to be more assertive, knowledgeable, and adaptable than ever before. Your parents could be more relaxed about certain educational matters. That does not mean that they were not strong advocates and not involved with their kids and schools. But schooling was more stable. It was there and that was that. They did not have to worry about school choice, safety, gang bullying, attendance, zero tolerance policies, and so on. In short, change and competition had yet not come to schooling. Now parents cannot tell who the players are without a program or understand all the performance measures without a scorecard.

5

DIAGNOSTICS: THE NEW PREDICTIVE SCIENCE

Schools have new and different ways of tracking and even labeling students. A kindergarten teacher, for example, can recommend, because a five-year-old does not know the entire alphabet, that he or she be taken out of class three times a week and put into a special Title I catch-up program. The authority of the teacher plus the availability of this special wonderful support program lead parents to acquiesce. But what parents are not told is that the Title I choice often is noted on the student's permanent record. Chances are that that record, plus routine teachers' comments to each other, especially in consultation with those teaching the next grade, will result in your kid being dubbed slow.

What are your options? What else can you do other than agree? Ask the teacher to specify exactly what your kid is expected to know, by what date, and how he or she will be tested on the alphabet. Then run your own Title I: teach your kids at home or get a tutor. Don't be buffaloed into being a partner in stigmatizing your kid.

Although parents know a lot about their kids, especially how they learn, their knowledge is often regularly ignored by teachers or listened to with only half an ear. Suddenly, a lively, restless chatterbox at home is perceived as hyper and disruptive in school. Teachers, especially anal types, want conformity and obedience. Toward those ends, schools have become triage centers.

The most difficult cases are identified, and they either shape up or are shipped out to an alternative school, which is where they send all the rotten apples before they spoil all the other good ones. At the other end of the spectrum are the restless kids. Before you know it, your kid's teacher is suggesting that your kid is too active and perhaps is suffering from ADD (Attention Deficit Disorder). It is important to note that this diagnosis is driven not by what the home but what the school values: attention and classroom management. Before you can recover from the shock, the teacher or counselor begins to describe some of the dire and long-term consequences of not attending to ADD now, and then gives the clincher: it is easy to remedy. There are a number of medications which can manage the hyperactivity. What they don't tell you is that the medications probably will turn your kid into a zombie.

ADD simply means that the kid has difficulty paying attention. He has a short attention span and is easily distracted, or he prefers to do geography when the class is doing math, or he acts up and disturbs other kids and distracts them from their studies. A number of decades ago when report cards had a whole section on conduct, such a kid might be marked for having behavior problems. At that point, many parents would usually do one of two things: discipline the kid, sometimes physically; or find some ways at home to help solve the problem of lack of focus.

Steven Spielberg, the movie producer, evidenced similar behavior problems. At that time, medications were not that available or prevalent. When the teacher talked to Mrs. Spielberg about it she quickly agreed; and she went on to describe how he stood on the coffee table, and made his mother and father go through certain dictated actions while he took moving pictures with his imaginary camera. The teacher and the mother sighed in shared exasperation and left it at that. Many years later when Spielberg was famous, his mother was interviewed and, asked to name what psychological approach she used for such antics, she responded simply, "I never said no."

Here is another example, perhaps the most dramatic. Thomas Edison's teacher called his mother to school and told her the boy was "addled." Today, that would rapidly designate a special education child, the precise definition of which would require extensive diagnostic testing. Often it designates a kid who in the past simply was called slow but now would be designated as special ed and having a below-average IQ.

Once again as with the wonderful Title I program, educators often offer a thoughtful way of handling the problem; it is called a Special Diploma. Parents sign and agree without being told that with such a diploma their kid cannot enter college or join the military. Inadvertently and with good intentions but deficient knowledge they may have signed away their kid's future.

After Mrs. Edison listened to her son's teacher, she immediately removed him from that school and taught him at home; and as they say, the rest is history. Mrs. Edison was ahead of her time. Now almost one million households are homeschooled. Those kids have won merit scholarships and national competitions and secured admissions to the colleges of their choice.

The common denominator of all these examples is parents not giving up on their kids. But that is not enough. They have to know more so that they can evaluate what the school is recommending and if necessary challenge it. They need to know the chain of command: who to go to, what to ask, what their rights are to information, and who has the authority to waive or alter what is sanctioned. If a teacher in the process resents such an active role of parents, they need to inform both the teacher and the principal that the actions and comments of that teacher will be monitored. Above all, parents need to look ahead and examine the long-term consequences of school decisions or recommendations. They should never allow themselves to be part of any process, no matter how well-intentioned, that prematurely limits the scope of the future options of their kids.

Some will object to such suspiciousness or militancy on the part of parents. They will point to many positive experiences with good and caring teachers and schools, and of course they would not only be right but also fortunate. In my defense though, I would advance three counterarguments.

First, there is a real need to contemplate worst-case scenarios, lest some parents may be pressured into making decisions they may later regret. Second, schools are becoming tougher and less patient than they used to be. Both teachers and administrators are increasingly and routinely on the defensive and even regularly maligned and battered. Just think of the knee-jerk rule of "Zero Tolerance." If parents operated on that principle most kids would not last six months. Given such conditions and environments, students can fall between the cracks. Some schools, determined to look good on state-mandated tests, have dropped special ed kids and/or bilingual classes from school tallies.

But third, even if none of the worst-case scenarios apply, and even if the teachers are all generally talented and student-centered, parents would still have to know more. School choice, for example, is no simple matter. To make an intelligent decision, parents have to know what are the differences between schools, a host of curricula options, whether teachers have a governance structure that provides them with access to decision making and to defining what constitutes student success, and so on and so on. In short, parents need to know what schools know.

Choice requires knowledge of what is going on generally in education and, equally as important, what is likely to be happening in the future. So parents have to know scope and extent: the big picture and what lies ahead.

Education is no longer all of a piece; it is a complex puzzle. In short, what is driving educational change has to become parents' knowledge base.

The obvious reason for the long term is that that is precisely the span of your kids' educational and work future. Every decision positions parents and kids for the next decision. Some educational decisions offer more, different, and better options than others, and those can be identified in advance and given priority.

So be patient. You will learn about schools, teachers, and administrators —perhaps, more than you may believe you have to know. But remember, you are not solely learning about education. Education is but the tip of the iceberg. What is happening to education is happening to everything else. The future of education contains in miniature the future of business, government, and the professions. What is driving educational change is driving all career choices. Tying it all together provides the best vantage point for making educational decisions and career directions.

6

FUTURE SCHOOL TRENDS

A law of escalation dominates forecasting. The future is available in three forms: future stretch, strain, and shock. The earlier the choice, the more options are available, and generally the more humane the options. However, if stretch is ignored, the next offering is strain, which provides fewer choices and less attractive ones. Finally, if that stage is rejected, there is shock, which is often grim and involves crisis management (a contradiction in terms). In short, openness and options ultimately are versions of each other.

One does not have to be a futurist to know that public education faces stretch, strain, and shock. For the next decade or more it will not be business as usual. Change will intrude often, and in ways that professional educators may intensely dislike. Sadly, perhaps, many defenders of the faith are prophets of the past, who are rallying the troops with angry and knee-jerk rhetoric. Most serious of all, they are fighting a rearguard action and their backs are facing the future. The value of a futurist, then, is that his or her descriptions of the trends generally are diagnostic; they tell not only what may happen, but also why and how. That's important because whatever changes or whichever interventions are contemplated, it is important not to replicate or create what has not worked or will encounter serious resistance both inside and outside the profession. The additional value is that futurists are never so presumptuous as to design a future that requires the kind of expertise only educators have. But on the basis of the way the future generally behaves as well as their expertise on the survivability and durability of certain options over others, futurists also can identify the "specs" for new designs.

DIAGNOSTIC TRENDS

There are five major trends that constitute the vital signs of education. Their impact individually and collectively is generally negative or not favorable to the future of education.

1. Effectiveness

Justified or not, and complexity notwithstanding, schools are perceived to be less effective now than they were in the past. Popular polls indicate that students do not know as much as they did before. Businesses claim they inherit graduates who do not know to read, write, and calculate; and they in turn have to spend millions to accomplish what the schools failed to. Community colleges follow suit by running extensive remediation programs. School safety and security have become a national priority with assaults on teachers and students increasing. Sensational examples of violence in the schools indicate that the environment is not a secure one. Over 50 percent of the teachers graduating from colleges of education do not enter the profession; and of those that do, over 50 percent do not stay beyond the first year. Thus, the public perception of education is its general inability to accomplish its fundamental mission. Indeed, if that were not the case, some of the other trends below would not be strong enough in their own right to remain threatening trends. However, education's condition is generally weak and unfavored. Other than educators themselves, public education has few defenders, allies, or constituencies.

2. Fragmentation

Public education generally has for many generations enjoyed a monopoly on education. To be sure, private and parochial schools always existed, but they were generally marginal to the entire educational sector. Now competition generally rules. There are nearly two million homeschoolers. Although that does not involve a loss in school budgets, homeschooling has drained off some of the brightest students and most committed parents. And now many have reached the point where they are winning national contests, emerging as National Merit Scholars, and gaining early admission to outstanding colleges and universities. Although charter schools so far evidence a mixed report, they are a more serious threat because they drain off per capita budget. There are nearly 2,000 charter schools currently operating with more on the way. California recently withdrew its restriction on the number of charter schools it would authorize to operate. Interestingly, many teachers are leaving public education to head up or teach in charter schools. There is also now a national organization that services charter schools (Mosaica).

Privatization is increasing. The Edison Project now involves about 100 schools; it plans to add another 200 this year and next. The evaluation of performance is mixed; this is a different form of competition because these are proprietary schools. They seek to produce a return on investment. Significantly, they are part of a national venture capital movement. Virtually all the new colleges and universities created during the last two decades have been for-profit institutions. They are designed to make money for their investors and are perceived as an important way to diversify a venture capitalist's portfolio. Unlike charter schools, these proprietary institutions have deep pockets and a proven track record.

Finally, various state voucher plans are nibbling at school enrollments and affecting teacher morale. In New Jersey failing schools are taken over by the state department of education and in effect become wards of the state and eligible for vouchers. In Florida, if a school fails the state skills test twice in a row, the state will offer vouchers to the parents to send their kids elsewhere. School choice is evidently faring better in the public's view than life choice.

3. Costs

This factor alone may be sufficient to have the entire education enterprise fall under its own weight. Education generally has been the only and most inflationary sector of the entire economy; there are no major or comprehensive efforts at cost containment. Productivity is defined in education as cost increase. Predictably each year taxes go up, just as college tuitions have increased scandalously to the point where many schools are now beyond the reach of the middle class. Demographic projections of the echo boom generation again typically have resulted in requests for funds to build or add on to existing buildings. The trend so far is that almost 90 percent of those requests will be rejected by the public, only 25 percent of whom have children in school in the first place. In many districts, more administrators than teachers have been added, with the net result that some teachers have not been rehired and class size has had to be increased. The combination of increased costs and questionable effectiveness is a double whammy that in business usually signals the demise of the company.

4. Technology

Everyone knows that education is labor intensive. But unlike in business, two solutions have not been used by schools: downsizing and technology. All the while public schools were becoming less effective, technology was becoming more effective. In fact, we now have a complete and deliverable high school curriculum, the high school in a box (including all AP courses). Professional associations like SALT (Society for Applied Learning Technology) run annual conferences at which state-of-the-art technology is described, demonstrated, and documented. In other words, we are no longer in the development stage; it is here, and tried and tested. However, the major obstacle is the taboo of replacement. Somehow we cannot bring ourselves to the politically incorrect acknowledgment that technology is no longer solely our handmaiden or our partner. It is equal to the task; it is as good as we are; it is our replacement. But the timeline is short on that recognition, because technological educational firms already are entering the public education market and servicing it. The same capitalistic energy, entrepreneurship, and competence that is operative in the privatization movement is also accomplishing significant inroads into public education. Here too many teachers are leaving a sinking ship to join and in some cases create education technology companies to service the instructional market.

5. Leaders as Martyrs

Unfortunately, education does not seem to be able to attract the kind of internal leadership to develop an action plan for the future. Instead of rallying educators to respond to the challenges of creating new school designs, unions are talking about increasing teacher salaries, lawyers are being retained to fight vouchers in the courts, professors of education are singing the songs of martyrdom and paranoia and attacking villainous business culture, and so on. Above all, what is needed is straight talk. Specifically, genuine leaders have to say the following: we have not been as effective as we have in the past; we may be indirectly responsible for the current fragmentation and maybe we should join and not resist it; we have not been good stewards of public trust and public funds; we should change our precious and defensive attitude toward technology and recognize that it may be the means for education to restore its former reputation of being effective, cost-conscious, and custom-tailored. Finally, we need to energize the profession so that we can regain control over our own destiny. Unless and until such honest confessions are made, and the current crop of doomsayers are rejected or ignored, the challenges of the future will remain stillborn, and education will have forsaken the option of being part of the incredible transformation of the twenty-first century.

7

THE FUTURE OF EDUCATION
AND THE FUTURE OF PARENTAL
INVOLVEMENT

The future of parental involvement cannot be discussed apart from the future of education. The latter in fact may determine the former. But what should be noted and even lamented at the outset is that educators defining the future of education often do not consult parents. If they are factored in at all, parents appear as a supplemental and token add-on. However, the argument here is that parental involvement is a central and seminal part of that future. By ignoring or slighting parental roles, educators may in fact be jeopardizing their capacity to achieve both their short- and long-term goals.

What will be different about education in the future and what do parents need to know about that difference, so that they and their kids will make better and more informed decisions about student success?

Six major trends will drive educational change:

I. ACCOUNTABILITY AND HIGH-STAKES TESTING

The next three decades will be dominated by three versions of accountability: higher standards, comprehensive measurement, and cost controls. The federal legislation of NCLB will require that such versions of accountability be applied nationwide, according to a prescribed timetable, and that schools exhibit adequate yearly progress or suffer the consequences. Although set up in stages and implemented gradually over a ten-year period, the legislation will totally transform education. The current generation of parents and students will uniquely be the objects of NCLB and embody future stretch, strain, and shock.

2. GLOBAL AND NATIONAL PRIORITY

Education increasingly will be perceived as a natural resource and professionals as a country's human capital. The economic competition between countries and cultures is being recast in the competition between educational systems. With the global economy increasingly taking hold and determining future careers, even national security will be defined in terms of world standings of educational performance. China already has projected its future in terms of the number of Olympic gold medals, Nobel Prize winners, and world-class concert virtuosos. Recently, Singapore identified ten areas of research excellence and launched a major recruiting and financial campaign to attract the brightest and the best from all over the world.

3. COMPETITION AND SCHOOL CHOICE

The dominant and almost monopolistic hold that public education, locally determined and traditional in form and delivery systems, has enjoyed for decades no longer applies. School choice, and the inevitable scramble for students and resources that follow in its wake, is education's new norm. Increasingly business is directly adding its competitive thrust into education as it seeks to garner market share of educational products and services. Every family everywhere now has an incredible number of options.

It can choose from an elaborate menu of homeschooling, regular public schools, parochial or private schools, charter schools, cyberschools, and so on. In addition, each choice may be followed by other choices. The student of the future may exhibit the same kind of educational range which later is likely also to characterize the number of career changes in their working lives. Finally, the prospect of vouchers in one form or another will facilitate and accelerate crossovers that many families never contemplated before. That will include the totally novel prospect of choosing a school operated by a for-profit private management company.

4. THE KNOWLEDGE WORKER AND THE KNOWLEDGE CULTURE

The future will see a shift from natural to intellectual resources, from financial to human capital, from brawn to brain, from labor to technology. In effect, the world is currently going through a second industrial revolution, except now it rests not on a factory but a knowledge base. Knowledge always has been power, but now it is not limited to an elite few but empowers workers to be managers who learn to work smarter, not harder. Over fifty corporate universities, which train over 100 million employees and cover over 100 countries and languages, have been created in the last ten years. Corporate universities are knowledge cultures whose aim is to produce knowledge workers who are able to be more productive and innovative and thus provide their organizations with a unique competitive edge and advantage.

5. THE DEMOGRAPHICS OF DIVERSITY, NATIONALLY AND GLOBALLY

By 2015, 40 percent of the school-age population will be non-Anglo in at least fifteen states. Major cities will be particularly impacted. In New York City, Miami, and Los Angeles, more than half the residents are immigrants or the children of immigrants. They come from close to 200 countries, speaking over 100 different languages, and there are no indications that the influx of legal or illegal immigrants is slowing. According to the most recent census, the largest minority population, one growing more rapidly than blacks, is Hispanic. In many areas of the country, they outnumber whites. When one adds the global religious

Moslem populations, it would not be inaccurate to claim that Caucasian Christians are an endangered species.

What all this means in terms of parents and their kids is advocacy for international education and cross-cultural programs. Study abroad programs should begin in high school and continue in college. Parents should be involved in student exchange programs and volunteer to be host families to foreign students. The reasons for all this are obvious: students today will be living, working, and moving in an incredibly diverse, interlocking, and interdependent world. Heterogeneity rather than homogeneity has to become their new comfort zone if they are to survive and prosper as working adults.

6. TECHNOLOGY AND DIGITAL FUTURES

Learning is replacing schooling. This is not semantics. Learning is no longer limited to schools or its schedule of time and place; it is now continuous, lifelong, and electronic. Courses are now prefixed as e-courses: e-economics, e-marketing, etc. The typical freshman college English course now requires that at least half of the research sources cited be electronic, and special forms of documentation have been developed for such citations. All the major universities that have been created since the end of WWII are distance education institutions enrolling adult learners. The Florida Virtual High School provides electronic courses to students all over the state, including AP courses to regions where there are not enough students to sustain an AP course.

However, according to experts the technological future will be more astounding and demanding. The projection is that the equivalent of 20,000 years of progress will occur in the first two decades of the twenty-first century. One of the major areas of change will be the new partnerships between human and computer intelligence and the general convergence of man and machine. Routinely, science fiction may be becoming science fact.

8

PARENTS' UNIVERSITY

How do these trends affect parents today and in the future? Minimally, three impacts are discernible:

I. A NEW EDUCATIONAL WORLD

The first is so obvious that it needs to be underscored. The extensive and radical changes in schooling will change the very definition of student success. At least three factors will shape that definition: school standards and testing, technological support, and parental roles and home environments.

2. NEW OPERATIONAL MODES AND MODELS

Parents will have to become planners. They will have to develop mid- and long-range strategic plans. A crucial component will be forging teacher-parent learning contracts and partnerships. Home and school ideally will evolve into a seamless relationship. Home environments will increasingly become computer- and Internet-based and optimize the use of the new electronic communication links established between home and school. Parents who are not computer-savvy or literate may have to take a course if they are to keep up with their kids and their technological educational options. In schools which provide computers at home, kids are required to teach parents as part of the payback.

3. A NEW PARENTS' EDUCATION PROGRAM

Because the future of everything is more of a challenge than ever before and compels new interactive relationships, parents need to change. Bridging the electronic generation gap and advocating international education as the means to diversity training and adaptation have already been noted. To those have to be added family negotiating skills, because school choice not only involves planning, but also dramatizes family values. Competition often leads parents into being intensely aggressive advocates for their kids. In Oakland, California, school choice was expanded to teacher choice, with the result that parents besieged the principal's office, demanding their first choice. In some cases that would mean a few teachers would be teaching 400 students each. The complex and new federal legislation of NCLB requires families to be knowledgeable about its requirements and provisions because they directly will impact their kids' performance. For example, the intense requirements of frequent testing may lead some parents to enroll their kids in test-taking prep courses locally or online. In short, parents need to go to back to school, but in this case to parents' college or university.

The course of study would be teacher–parent relationships. But who would provide the training? Would it be an offering of the school or the local PTA? If the latter, does it make sense for it to exclude direct participation by teachers? After all, the changes required are relational; both sides have to adjust for anything meaningful to develop. Moreover, how would the problem of intense advocacy by parents be restrained? They always push their own kids and often their own agenda or vendetta. Finally, can the workshop ever be totally inclusive? Parents are all different. Who they are is also determined by what stage they and their kids are at. Then, too, schools vary enormously, as do the principals and teachers. What works with one school may make no headway with another. Can one-size-fits-all really be successful?

All these questions already have been raised, addressed, and to a large extent solved by parents, schools, and teachers across the country.

Rather than reinvent the wheel, the first matter to discuss, not unlike the research on student success factors, is what has been done, how, why, and with what results.

DEFINING ROLES, PAST AND FUTURE

The first step is inventory: what have been the traditional and historical roles of parents? Although the list may vary somewhat depending on whether it is being compiled by teachers or by parents, generally it would include the same three key roles: supporters of the school and the curriculum; fund-raisers; and implementers of recommendations for student changes requested by teachers. In other words, in the past parents were expected to be essentially passive, obedient, and not involved. Like children they were to be seen, not heard. Parental involvement appeared to be an oxymoron like crisis management. It was defined more by what parents did not do than by what they did, and by the respectful distance they maintained; and generally it worked because schools in the past worked.

My parents treated teachers not just with respect but with reverence. They could do not wrong. If a teacher raised an issue about me, I was immediately judged to be guilty. The only question was the nature of the punishment, which would always be slightly worse than the teacher recommended. The absolute operating rule was: never argue, question, or disagree with the teacher. She was always right. Besides, the fear was that she would take it out on the kid and make matters worse. (Sadly, that was often true.)

My wife and I were different parents. We often questioned and even challenged curriculum, instruction, and administration; school board meetings were often contentious. Some parents played political PTA games so that they could be cozy with the teachers of their kids. Their Christmas presents were exceptionally generous. Kids were still fearful of retaliation; they evidently had seen it happen. In short, my generation of parents, unlike the current group of parents, did not really break new ground or carve out new roles. What most of us did discover often too late is that if any change is to occur it has to involve both teachers and parents. We left, in other words, the problem of restructuring mutuality to the present generation of parents.

THE DYNAMICS OF THE RELATIONSHIP

Negotiating a new arrangement between parents and teachers involves aspiration and need, respectively. The current generation of parents—the "Yes, but" group—seeks stronger, more involved roles. In addition, their support and fund-raising is increasingly conditional. It varies with the degree of their involvement, and it functions as a quid pro quo.

Educators are aware of the extent to which NCLB focuses on parent and student benefits more than those of educators. With data tracking of tests and the issuance of school report cards, educators increasingly find themselves in a fishbowl. If their students fail to make adequate yearly progress over time, schools can be taken over and even closed, and they may find themselves unemployed—an unexpected fate for a profession that historically always promised job security. At the same time, many educators have been persuaded—and the research confirms this—that they would have greater difficulty achieving and sustaining the higher standards, especially according to the timetable, without the involvement of parents. So aspiration and need came together and formed a more common purpose and focus. It often begins with both parties discussing prospective future parental roles.

INVOLVEMENT, PARTNERSHIP, AND LEADERSHIP: THE NEW ROLES

Parental involvement is a given. There is no going back; current versions of involvement generally enjoy greater scope. Partners and leaders are new roles; they increasingly may become the new norms of the future.

The extent of each role would vary with the school, region of the country, and its demographics. The same variety also would characterize the extent to which each one of the three would flow into and became the next one. But surprisingly, in spite of all the variables there is considerable national commonality.

The first matter all schools and parent groups share is the recognition that each role projects a spectrum. Specifically, each ranges from the minimum, to the maximum, to the optimum. Thus, parents can choose what is appropriate for them at any particular time and place and for each child. Also, as each role reaches its optimum point, it generally shifts to the next one. Thus, parents would gradually be prepared for and trained for assuming more demanding roles. Most important, teachers and parents have separately and mutually to review their perceptions of each other and the roles they have played, which may require both groups to alter their mindsets.

Here in matrix form are the roles spelled out in terms of activities:

	Involvement	Partnership	Leadership
ACTIVITY	MINIMUM	MAXIMUM	OPTIMUM
Information	Limited	Extensive	Total
Control	Unilateral	Shared	Reciprocal
Goals	Reviewed	Reaffirmed	Revised
Attitudes	Supportive	Questioning	Challenging
Money	Fund-Raisers	Foundations	Community Resource Developers
Perception	Consumers	Customers	Colearners

OBSTACLES

In the process of working out new relationships, certain obstacles may emerge on the part of both groups. Teachers are fearful that they would lose control, that parents would take over and boss them around and assume an expertise they did not have and, worst of all, primarily push for their own kids' advancement and advantage. Parents in turn do not want to be treated as dummies or servants, ignorant of the educational process and situation, or not invited to share their significant knowledge about their kids and their learning styles with teachers.

What generally has emerged from the interaction and negotiation to overcome these obstacles are a number of mutual insights:

1. Reciprocity has to become the operative and defining common goal.
2. Teachers have to regard parents as learning partners.
3. What teachers know about each kid has to be joined with what parents know. In effect, they became co-teachers.
4. The learning goals teachers sought for each student not only have to be shared with each parent, but also developed mutually—how

those goals can be achieved both in school and at home. In effect they became co-guiders.

5. Parental advocacy for one's own child has to be recast and redirected by teachers into advocacy for learning in general for all kids. No one is an island unto himself. Raising the level of the water raises the level of all ships. Particular school reforms should not be championed that benefit only certain kids or involve winners and losers. Parents and teachers have to find a new high road, together; they have to be co-advocates.

With reciprocity as the guideline, teachers and parents have to ask the following key questions (Lambert 2002):

- What do teachers and parents uniquely have to give and receive from each other?
- What do they have to learn from each other?
- What can they create together that did not exist before and that cannot be created apart from each other?
- How will teachers and parents be different after they have worked together and developed new relationships?
- In what ways will students evidence and benefit from these new working relationships?
- What will be the signs of student change and success?

ROLE OF TEACHERS IN CREATING AND EMPOWERING PARENT COMMUNITIES

Because in many ways educators historically more than parents have not encouraged parental participation or limited it to token roles or functions, the initiative for change may have to come from the school. To stir, stimulate, and structure the new relationships, the following ten guidelines should be developed by and for schools:

1. Develop and state explicitly the schools minimum, maximum, and optimum expectations of parents' participation.

2. Engage parents directly and actively from the start to be part of defining those expectations.
3. Develop a shared vision and mission. Schedule teacher–parent forums.
4. Make the daily workings of learning available and transparent. Develop an open school policy: no secrets, no evasion; total information sharing.
5. Share learning: bring together how students learn in school, and how they learn at home.
6. Set mutual role goals: each teacher a better teacher, each parent a better parent.
7. Facilitate parent input and development. Conduct focus groups, develop phone opinion surveys, etc.
8. Don't skirt tough or controversial issues. Ask for and expect to receive direct and candid input and even disagreement.
9. Keep dialogue broad based and generic so that as many parents as possible can be involved on the one hand, and the single-agenda parent and individual child advocacy can be avoided, on the other.
10. Ask parents to define their roles as partners and leaders and to summarize and assess their leadership experiences and skills.

SAMPLE PROGRAMS THAT HAVE PROMOTED PARENT PARTNERSHIP AND LEADERSHIP

Parents in turn and often separately have to develop their own guidelines and explore with each other their roles. However, characteristically parents talk less and act more. Here then are some examples of how parents have altered and expanded their roles:

1. Co-teaching in Gehanna, Ohio: Parents are trained as reading tutors working closely in a team of two students and one adult discussing in detail a nonfiction book they all read. The favorable ratio of nearly one on one has produced excellent results impossible without parents.

2. Advocacy Projects in Manitoba, Canada: Developing innovative problem-solving skills of both parents and students to address the difficult issues the schools face. Many solutions emerged.

3. Protocol Conversations in Walnut Creek, California: Parents, teachers, and students openly and candidly participate in the kind of conversations that typically take place in the review of student work or the exchanges in parent–teacher conferences. Not only did greater transparency reign, but the levels of discussion and exchange were raised.

4. Parent–Teacher Conferences in Calgary, Canada: Parents wanted to experiment with different formats for the traditional exchange. The one that produced the best results for both teachers and parents were those that were student-led and -scripted.

5. Parent Exchange Service in Los Angeles: The need for parents to help each other out with baby-sitting, picking up kids at school, shopping for an ailing parent, overnight stays during a family emergency, and so on, evolved into a formal Parent Exchange Service. Parents became not just a group but a community.

6. Parents University in Glassbrook Elementary School: Surveys of parents indicated that 90 percent expected their kids to go to college, but confessed that they did not have the information they needed to help their kids get there. Also, although parents read about brain research and new developments in technology, they were unsure what they meant and how they applied to their kids. So Parents University was formed to provide professional development workshops for both teachers and parents together.

The above is but a partial list of the kind of creative collaboration and results that can emerge when teachers and parents become involved with, partner with, and lead each other. The descriptions here do not in any way exhaust all possibilities or what may emerge in the future. However, it is easy to be carried away by success. It is also necessary to be realistic and to address two downsides.

The first has to do with the very real prospect that school, teachers, and administrators currently may be at a stage where they are not receptive to greater parental involvement but the parents are. What do parents do then? The second reality check involves the general lack of time for teachers to co-plan lesson follow-up with parents.

ADJUSTING PARENTAL ROLES TO SCHOOL RECEPTIVITY

Although where schools are at can be defined according to different criteria, a unique classification is to judge schools by the degree of parent involvement. Thus, using and adapting Lambert's categorization of schools into four types or quadrants, how does each perceive and use parents? And what adjustments are required to bring about a reasonable fit, so as not to create animosity between school and parents and frustrate the good intentions of parents?

1. Quadrant I Schools

The school is self-contained and faces inwardly. The principal may rule like a feudal lord, and teacher governance is limited. Little has changed over the years. If the demographics are favorable, they may believe they do not have to change; they also may believe they will not have any difficulty meeting all the requirements of NCLB.

In such a school few parents are involved. When they are, it is usually to press for the best teacher for their child. Otherwise, except for being called to school for a discipline problem, parents' voices are generally silent. Would such a school benefit from greater school involvement? Of course. But parents might be spinning their wheels. Little progress can be made if the school is unwilling or secretly opposed to opening the doors wider to parents. School attitude is thus crucial. Parents can still of course seek to help their kids be successful in school, but it would be an individual, not a mutual or community effort.

2. Quadrant II Schools

Such a school is usually in transition, especially when neighborhoods change their demographics or SES, or a new principal arrives; but if the majority of teachers are older and/or the principal's tenure long, change and openness may be limited, tentative, and partial. If they encounter the shock waves of NCLB, their basic initial responses will take the form of band-aids and fast and dirty fixes. They will avoid as long as they can looking more deeply into causes rather than symptoms. However, if the school district is energized by a newly elected school board or a new superintendent with a mandate for change, the Quadrant II School may be dragged into the twenty-first century. But before that happens, or if it does not happen, parental access is restricted.

Although more parents are involved in such a school, it tends to be limited to school life and extracurricular areas such as sports teams or the performing arts. In effect, parents are expected to be team boosters or cheerleaders. They raise money for school trips or to send the choral group to perform in Orlando or London. They also may act as chaperones; but generally they are excluded from academics. Symptomatically, the school has not introspectively engaged the issue of parent participation. It would be an uphill battle for parents to hasten the process. They may have to wait for NCLB and other pressures to soften such schools up and lead them out of denial.

3. Quadrant III Schools

These schools have been led by enlightenment or top-down orders to change their ways and to become more parent- and community-focused and involving. In this case, the chicken-egg and push-pull processes are already at work. Both the school and the parents see eye to eye and are pushing for the same ends. As a result, what is clearly established is the recognition that parent participation is not only a parental but also a school goal.

In such schools, parents become more focused and active. Responsibility for school improvement becomes a shared responsibility. Teachers and parents become partners.

4. Quadrant IV Schools

These are the kinds of schools that produced many of the creative activities and new directions sampled above. Because reciprocity rules, parents can—and frequently do—become leaders. Such schools are future labs; they are ahead of their time. Happily their existence and their parental accomplishments serve as models for other, less advanced, schools; but it is still sobering to remember that even with such schools, parent leadership may have been the last area to be addressed.

PARENT LEADERSHIP ON BEHALF OF SCHOOL REFORM

Parent leadership sometimes also has been generic and not solely school- or child-specific. In fact, it may have to be systemic and structural, and it may even have to address the teacher culture. It always has to be proactive. Parents have to ask, What about the way school is organized and teachers operate stands in the way of certain kinds of change that parents advocate from happening?

Take, for example, the issue of partnerships and knowledge sharing between teachers and parents. It is not enough to come to a new arrangement, significant though that breakthrough may be, it if is still-born or a frustratingly catch-as-catch-can process. It is at this point where parents have to step back and link their leadership to knowledge of the way things work and what is needed.

Minimally, there are two formidable obstacles. The first is the general teacher culture of isolation. The second is the tyranny of the typical school schedule.

Teachers are basically lone rangers. They close their doors and value being totally in charge. Students rightly complain that teachers give out homework as if their class was the only one students are taking. When did teachers ever share, let alone coordinate, assignments or test dates with other teachers? It does not happen. The teacher culture precludes or at least does not support it, yet the research urges and documents collaboration.

In Japan the school day is lengthened to give students opportunity for more physical exercise and to facilitate the collaborative lesson planning of teachers. Teachers of the same grade level or subject area, or both, meet. Each member of the group presents his daily and weekly lesson plan, and the group discusses and critiques the plan. It raises questions about the goals, the methodologies proposed, and suggests alternatives, identifies resources and research findings, and so forth. The result is always a much improved, focused, and usually more successful plan. If the teacher wishes to preserve the fiction that she did it all by herself and still reign supreme as the lone ranger when she closes her door, she can do so; but she is more likely to conceive of her teaching in collaborative than isolationist terms. That may be buttressed if the teacher group also collectively addresses the review of students' work. That arrangement not only obviously benefits students but also helps define student success and clarify school goals and their alignment with classroom goals. When one adds the need for teachers and parents also to collaborate it may be like the proverbial straw that breaks the camel's back.

The issue is how to find the time not only for parent partnerships to work but also for the entire collegial process to alter the basic teacher culture of isolation. The issue of time seems so intractable that that alone may be the reason for the isolation of teachers in the first place, and the lack of bridges between teachers and parents in the second place. It may have less to do with internals than with externals, less involved with motivation than with mechanisms. After all, the Japanese lengthened the day.

To bring about such significant cultural and systemic change may especially require parental leadership for at least two reasons. First, it is a compelling priority. It would improve the performance of teachers and their kids. Second, parents are not party to the system or its culture and thus may have fresh eyes and bring another perspective to solving the problem. In other words, they are not locked in and may be able to think outside of the box. They may be able to convert absolutes into variables. Above all, they are determined to find a solution, which is what always characterizes leadership. Where there is a will there is a way.

A good creative approach is the leapfrog concept: while we are catching up let us also get ahead. Time needs to be found to accomplish three critical tasks: collaborative teacher planning; collective review of student work; and teacher partnerships to develop and design follow-up home assignments. In fact, all three stages should be perceived as a continuum. Lesson planning would also include individualized homework planning; the review of student work would generate precise rubric profiles of strength and areas of improvement, which also could be shared with and worked on by parents. A seamless and holistic process involving all the critical stakeholders could be put in place.

Parents might question why subject matter classes have to meet five days a week. If they instead were scheduled three times, on MWF for example, that would leave TTh open. The immediate and knee-jerk objections would involve covering the curriculum and supervision. But students would not be abandoned at that time or expected to work on their own. Students would be grouped into study teams; they would be given group lesson plans and goals to be accomplished. Peer tutoring would be provided. Computer programs would be designated and integrated. Follow-up at home through group e-mails and chat rooms also would be set up. Groups that goofed off or fooled around, wasted time, or played video games on the computer would be in for a rude group shock when they failed their group tests and each member received the group grade of F.

Would it work? It already has. Research has confirmed the value and even quantum leaps of peer tutoring. Computer drilling has been more effective and less punitive than using more expensive teachers as drill sergeants. Collaborative group learning not only has proved to be productive, but also anticipates later functioning in work teams, especially when strengthened by including negotiating and conflict resolution skills. Historically, law students have bailed out generations of law students with study teams, and college coaches have routinely used study tables for their athletes after dinner. In short, the cause, the commitment, and the creative solution are ready-made for parental leadership. In fact, if they do not make it their mission it may not happen; but if they do and it does happen, then that will signal a new day not only for schools, but also for parents as partners and leaders. Finally, all committed to improving the quality of education also would recognize that parent participation has become not only a central object of but also an agent for school reform.

Part 3

FRAMEWORKS AND RELATIONSHIPS

Clearly, it is important for parents to know what is happening to education and how it may affect the future learning, life, and work of their children. Sadly, it is equally important for parents to recognize the capacity of schools to introduce and even to indoctrinate failure, so that they can be diagnostically vigilant about its terrible signs on the one hand, and take corrective action and interventions by asserting parents' rights and entitlements on the other. Above all, parent participation in schools and partnerships with educators now and increasingly in the future are likely to become a permanent fixture and feature of school reform. However, now it is necessary to turn to another set of basics: the learning relationships between parents and their children. To set the stage for that it may be helpful to invoke and use a special inclusive and enriched learning framework. The one recommended here is that of Howard Gardner's multiple intelligences.

9

THE HOLISTICS OF
MULTIPLE INTELLIGENCES (MI)

Wordsworth's earliest collection of poems—to some still his best—was his *Lyrical Ballads* (1798). Even the title quietly sought to break new ground. Ballads were supposed to be long and generally unmusical narratives, but Wordsworth created ballads that told a story, were unusually short, and offered the kind of musicality associated with lyrics. That combination of story and song in fact appropriately supported his many poems about children. One in particular, "We are Seven," carries us rapidly and deeply to the theme of this chapter.

The poem is an exchange between an adult and a child. It begins casually and calmly with the adult inquiring about the child's family. The answer is that there are seven children in the family. However, further pressing by the adult reveals that two are dead and another two are away in the city. Invoking arithmetic, the adult then disputes the oft-repeated claim by the child that "we are seven." Finally, the adult becomes angry and frustrated. He subtracts the two who are dead and the two who are away and hopes that will clinch his argument that in fact they are not seven but three, but to no avail. The child holds firm. The adult finally relents, but not before conceding that sometimes there is more wisdom in children than is acknowledged by adults.

Like all Romantic writers, Wordsworth invested children with special power and even role reversal. The adult in the poem recovers his own childhood and in the process also acquires the special and double knowledge of the child-adult. In particular, the wisdom of the child in "We Are Seven" is holistic. His view of his family is intact; it preserves its original totality. It is not subject to the laws of addition or subtraction. In his mind's eye, his absent brothers and sisters are all there together, and always will be.

The minds of adults are ruled by parts, not wholes. Growing up, we are taught to break down everything into its constituent parts. As Wordsworth later warned, "We murder to dissect." Learning generally is a process of separating what initially was and perhaps should always remain united. By holding the more encompassing vision of children up to the separatist and analytical minds of adults, Wordsworth was trying to encourage in his *Lyrical Ballads* an act of recovery—of persuading adults to go back in time and recover the gift of holistic vision of their childhood. Wordsworth's own version was to keep alive the child within him as an adult.

That recalls the famous response of Picasso to the standard accusation that his paintings could have been done by a three-year-old: "Of course. But that is no great accomplishment for a three-year-old. But it is quite another matter for a man who is forty-three to be able to paint like a three-year-old!"

What is preserved and gained by keeping the child alive within an adult? What to Wordsworth and Picasso is the essence of childhood? It is the ability to see things whole. Perception is not separate from what is perceived. Subject and object are one: I see the tree and the tree sees me. Things outside do not remain external but cooperate in their being mutually perceived; in other words, the child contains the world in miniature. He is of a piece with his environment. The whole always involves the imagination of always keeping things together. The child has vision.

However, growing up involves the learning of separation. Objects and subjects are not one and the same. I see the tree, but the tree is inanimate and does not see me. There is always gain and loss. The loss of unity and the mutual perception of me and tree are offset, however, by the gain that the child can now analyze and learn more about that object as a separate entity. That gap enables science to enter and supplement the child's imagination. The only problem is that in our haste to have kids grow up and to protect them from unreality, we tend to throw the baby out with the bathwater. Imagination is minimized or even ridiculed. A child's way of thinking is stigmatized and cast off in order to be replaced gradually by acquiring grown-up ways of thinking and learning. Unlike the model offered by Wordsworth and Picasso, parents and teachers, and parents as teachers, often do not seek the more complicated and enriched goal of keeping both imagination and analysis alive together, interactive, and coexistent within the growing and learning child. Indeed, the crucial time for that to happen is at home during the preschool years.

Happily, along comes Howard Gardner, an educational psychologist, who not only lauds the wholeness of children, but also describes the richness it contains. Gardner claims that there is not just one kind of intelligence measured by IQ tests but multiple intelligences (MI), and further, that all exist in embryonic form in childhood. Suddenly what we intuitively knew was confirmed: that there are many different ways of knowing—that in fact there are different strokes for different folks.

In other words, MI establishes multiple access. If one door does not open there are always others. Versatile teachers and parents often talk about their bag of tricks. It would be more accurate to refer to it as a MITK, Multiple Intelligence Tool Kit. In addition, there are preferred ways of knowing. Some children have special strengths. Some are highly visual or spatial, while others are musical or involve physical movement. There are also cultures where people are more vocal or use their hands and bodies to communicate. When parents reflect back on what their grown-up kids were as children, they frequently will say, "She was always acting things out" or "He was always arranging things." Sometimes they lament not encouraging those alternatives more.

Gardner urges teachers to recognize and to tap the multiple intelligences particularly available in children. That way students with different but no less powerful ways of comprehending and communicating can benefit from a differentiated approach. If the goal is to leave no child behind, no better system than MI could be found for that comprehensive end. In effect, Gardner has replaced and endowed the earlier notion of different learning styles with scientific rigor. But the value of Gardner may be more important for parents than for teachers, for at least three reasons:

1. From birth, parents have an access that teachers do not. They witness the child's development. Most first-time parents are concerned initially with its being normal like every other child; but

once that is assured they perceive a double pattern. One follows the general evolutionary line of all children, the other the individual variations of the child. The first stems from his being normally human, the second from his being normally multiple.

2. Parents need to prize the holistic imagination of their kids and seek to keep it alive and not at odds with analysis. The child should not be prematurely prepared and shaped for school, which in fact more often than not is a place of narrowing rather than expanding choices. In other words, the parent as the child's first teacher and the home as his first school should be devoted to preserving, not reducing, multiple intelligences. The child will be better equipped with and amplified by a larger whole to sustain later learning in school. Keeping the imagination of the child alive will also benefit and contribute to his success as a working adult and prepare him later for being an effective parent.

3. Parents should resist premature or partial specialization of the way kids learn. Don't always buy them only the same kind of toys or videotapes. Don't join the herd and purchase what everyone has been persuaded by TV ads to acquire. Don't encourage only a certain kind of play. In other words, review frequently Gardner's multiple intelligences and be guided by them. Perceive your child as the hub of a wheel, with many spokes and strokes emerging and enriching that center. In short, perceive the multiplicity within and inherent in the whole child.

GARDNER'S LIST OF MULTIPLE INTELLIGENCES

What are the different kinds of intelligences according to Gardner? When he originally published his *Frames of Mind* (1983), he listed seven. He later added an eighth. I have taken the liberty of adding a ninth. The descriptions below are accompanied by careers associated with each intelligence.

1. Linguisitic Intelligence

Reading, writing, and talking—all the skills of communication through language, texts, and dialogue. In current cultures this is the dominant form of intelligence. It is raised to high levels of preeminence by professional writers, literary artists, editors, and broadcast specialists.

2. Physical/Bodily and Kinesthetic Intelligence

The ability to use one's body and its skills to communicate and to create. It includes athletes, actors, mimes, dancers, sculptors, and craftsmen of all kinds.

3. Spatial Intelligence

Visualizing power in general and visual thinking and organizing in particular. Examples include architects, mapmakers, graphic artists, and inventors.

4. Musical Intelligence

Sensitivity and receptivity to sound, rhythm, beat, melody, and so on, developed professionally by musicians, singers, and composers.

5. Logical and Mathematical Intelligence

Facility with numbers and patterns, and abstract concepts and categories, characteristic of scientists, physicians, computer programmers, and statisticians.

6. Intrapersonal Intelligence

Access to emotions, capacity to understand and express inner feelings, empathy for others, and ability to apply that sympathy and internal understanding to the lives of others. Examples include salesmen, psychotherapists, social workers, religious leaders, and so on.

7. Interpersonal Intelligence

Strong awareness of the ways individuals and groups relate, and how they persuade, manipulate, affect, and motivate each other, typical of teachers, union organizers, human resources professionals, administrators, pollsters, and politicians.

8. Naturalist Intelligence

Sensitivity and knowledge of the natural environment and its creatures. Finds expression in careers as biologists, ecologists, veterinarians, farmers and breeders, forest rangers, and so on.

9. Futuristic/Anticipatory Intelligence

Ability to look ahead, to be proactive, to engage in what is yet to be, to ask constantly the question, "What if?" Characteristic of inventors, science fiction writers, strategic long-range planners and forecasters.

Before going any further with the analysis, it might be helpful to test the value of MI as a diagnostic tool by applying the nine categories, first to yourself, and then to one of your kids.

First, using a scoring system from 0 to 10, estimate the strength or extent of each category. Then assign the grade you received in school in general for each category. Also include a career choice if it applies. Finally tally and evaluate.

Second, ideally select a kid who already has been in school long enough to try out the various intelligences and to accumulate enough grades to generate an average grade. In the career column list what career directions are indicated by the scores recorded.

Me	Score	Grade	Career Choice
1. Linguistic			
2. Physical			
3. Spatial			
4. Musical			
5. Mathematical			
6. Intrapersonal			
7. Interpersonal			
8. Naturalist			
9. Futurist			

Highest Scores
Grade/Career Correlation or Lack of it

My Kid	Score	Grade	Career Direction
1. Linguistic			
2. Physical			
3. Spatial			
4. Musical			
5. Mathematical			
6. Intrapersonal			
7. Interpersonal			
8. Naturalist			
9. Futurist			
Tally			

CAREER DIRECTIONS

Now comes the fun part: applying MI at home and school, but first at home.

10

APPLYING MULTIPLE INTELLIGENCES AT SCHOOL AND HOME

When parents are asked to go back in time and think about their kids when they were very young, they invariably include in their list of qualities their curiosity (which sometimes led them into trouble) and their self-absorption in learning (so intense often that they forgot to go to the bathroom). Or if one watches an infant using the language and thinks of her hands reaching out to objects, people, or pets, or the busy play of prekindergartners, the same drive to know and to experience is amply in evidence.

Then they go to school. For many kids not only has their world changed but often so have they. They are often now more serious, sometimes glum. The only time they seem as happy as before is when they play games with their friends. But in school they learn to worry. They develop an almost military respect for rules and chain of command. They may show early signs of sadness, perhaps the kid's version of depression and the early stages of terminal failure.

Others may be bubbly and happy about school. They also tend to be very serious about everything about school: keeping their book bag orderly, getting their homework done, and urging parents to sign and return stuff on time. They also may have made new friends with whom they have play dates. Those kids choose peers because inevitably schooling introduces hierarchy.

Perhaps for the first time, kids learn their place and standing in the pecking order of achievement. Parents who think their kids are bright are saddened by conversations about who is the smartest or scores the highest grades in the class. When the parents assert that their kid is smart, the kid replies philosophically, "Yes, but not as smart as Neil or Mary." Often that is followed by a further explanation of what kind of math genius Mary is.

So school is both a continuation and departure from home. Happy kids from happy homes are often happy in school. Unhappy kids from unhappy homes sometimes flourish in school. Even though it is fashionable in the culture to hate school, they do not; for them it is a place of rescue, a positive contrast to an often not very positive home. However, for others who come from happy homes, school is not a happy place. For them and for their parents, school and the home are at odds. As Glasser noted, if the gulf remains or gets bigger, and if it lasts until the age of ten, it is likely to be permanent.

Is there any way to predict which kids will thrive in school and which ones will not? Partly so. But even if that were possible, is there any way to schoolproof kids so that they avoid failure on the one hand and enjoy success on the other? Yes and no. There are many things parents can do, but there are certain don'ts.

One don't is to live your life through that of your children. Another is to fail to develop independence early on. Parents who give a child a task to do, and then impatiently take it away and finish it themselves, create a child who is likely to grow up with completion deficiency. As adults they cannot seem to finish reports on time. They generally have difficulty meeting deadlines or coming to closure, and they routinely lead incomplete or unfinished lives.

The problem with obsessing about the threat of failure is that it may function as a self-fulfilling prophecy on the one hand, and an enormous disservice to many kids who thrive in school on the other. Even the more modest approach of risk reduction may introduce fears that are paralyzing or unrealized. Parents often overcompensate. Providing every conceivable stimulating and learning device promoted by enterprising providers may be overkill. They also may develop learning pathways and expectations at odds with those of the school. They also are frequently so realistic, detailed, and developed that they impoverish the imagination. My favorite toy as a kid was a clothespin (which obviously dates me because most kids today don't know what a clothespin is).

So what course of action seems best? The following basic orientations:

- The home is the child's first school.
- Parents are his first teachers.
- Every family thus is involved in homeschooling.
- In some cases that also becomes for certain families their later schooling choice.
- In all cases, home as school and parents as teachers never end.

Although there are inevitably many varied and different kinds of home and parental teaching styles possible, about which many hold passionate views, we are going to focus only on MI (Multiple Intelligences), because that is currently the only system that preserves the whole child on the one hand and his rich interior of multiple potentials on the other. It is also the only learning approach that is in harmony with Glasser and his Choice Therapy. There are however a few guiding essentials and principles that sensibly apply to all learning systems on the one hand but are especially optimized by Gardner (1983) and Glasser (1998) on the other:

1. Safety.
2. Talk.
3. Play.
4. Never saying no.
5. Always offering choices (Glasser).

I. SAFETY

This is an absolute. Always survey the scene indoors or outdoors, neighborhood, playgrounds, places kids frequent and families visit, and so on, for danger signs. This especially true when kids ride bikes or later drive cars. The parental role here is that of zero tolerance: no debates, no negotiation. Be short, direct, and tough. This is an action, not a discussion item.

2. TALK

Classrooms should be busy and noisy; so should homes. Silence can be deadly and palling. The TV or radio should not be the only or dominant sound. Families that eat and talk together stay together. Hopefully, the days of children being seen but not heard are over. Still, in some homes parents and kids often do not communicate. This is a particular problem as kids grow older; teenagers in particular can talk for hours on the phone but regularly give parents the silent treatment. But ways have to be found to dialogue.

Glasser talks to teachers about the difficulties of breaking the ice and getting kids to talk openly and candidly. One of his characteristic solutions is to talk only about tough subjects such as lying, cheating, bullying, dropping out of school, unhappiness, being poor, and so on.

When families place a high value on talking to each other, they can be surprisingly creative. Some families create traditions at mealtime in which different members rotate taking the lead and pick a current event to discuss. Others invoke "The Family Huddle" when a subject involving everyone needs to be talked over or a problem solved. Some families create special car games when traveling. In short, where there is a will there is a way. When parents value conversation they will find ingenious ways to make it happen. Actually, talk is not only a daily investment in the future of the family and its well-being; it is also the best investment in the future of their kids' performance in school. Kids who are accustomed to talking, and asking and answering questions, are a teacher's delight.

3. PLAY

To children play and learning are the same thing. In fact, the power of play to engage, absorb, and instruct knows no age bounds. Working adults attend workshops that feature imagined situations or simulations. Frequently, participants are asked to role play; managers assume the role of workers or customers. Complex long-range plans are accompanied by scenarios. The famous Harvard MBA program is built on narrative case studies.

The capacity of children to play imaginative games, live in created worlds, construct elaborate Lego or Erector Set models, be absorbed in video games, and so on, is beyond question. Sadly, these are mostly home, not school, activities. In this instance at least school should imitate the home, but school often derides play and principals devalue teachers who use it. Children are lectured that school is serious business. It is work. It represents their job. They are regularly warned that it is a jungle out there, and they are being prepared to face and survive that tough world. The only problem is that by setting learning and play at odds with each other, the school may turn out to be such a grim place that a jungle would be preferable. The enemy is not outside but inside the gates. Examples of keeping play alive—keeping the child alive within—can be found below for each intelligence.

4. NEVER SAYING NO

This response recommended for parents as teachers is also a key principle of excellent customer service (in other words, treat your kids as you would like to be treated as a customer). Good customer service representatives are taught never to say no, especially if that is in fact the final answer. The first wrong answer is "This is the company policy." (Mother to child: "That kind of behavior is unacceptable in this home. It may be OK in your girlfriend's home but not here!") The second wrong answer is "This is your fault. You screwed up, we didn't." (Father to teenager: "What were you thinking? Where were your brains? Well, you have to bite the bullet and take the blame for this one.") And so on.

Good customer representatives and parents take another tack: "Well let us see what we can do. Let us first try to understand how this all came about. Take me through the steps as best as you can remember them. Explain what led you to make certain decisions and why that made sense to you at the time."

Inquiry replaces accusation. Although a wrong does not finally end up being a right, how a kid got there is critical knowledge not only for this problem, but for reprogramming to avoid other problems. Indeed, that is where parents have to go. Customer and child retention are the goals of the game. If condemnation is finally involved, let it be the sin rather than the sinner.

5. ALWAYS OFFERING CHOICES

It is here where customer service representatives and parents may have to part company. The reps finally may have few or no solutions to offer: consolations, yes, but they cannot give away the store. However, parents are never without resources as long as they also do not ever give up on their kids. The parents who give up early in the game, who use ultimatums and back kids into corners, have lost the game before it begins. According to Glasser, choices are always available. Recovery or new directions are always possible. Parents and kids should never be at a dead end or reach a point of no recall; in fact, the goal of Choice Therapy is never to go there.

Instead of characteristically telling kids what to do or what you think, transfer the options for action and change to kids. They can be highly directive—"You have two choices here: you can either do this or do that"—or invitational: "What choices do you believe you have in this situation?" (If the answer is none and under prodding and prompting it remains that way, parents always can go back to the directive style.)

The teacher or parent has not surrendered control or final decision making. That is kept in reserve. Once the choices are spelled out, and a final course of action is agreed upon by both parent/teacher and kid, then, following the Glasser model, is when the really important parental/teacher roles kick in. Three key questions are asked: "Are you committed to follow this route?," "Are there any ways that I or we can help you to get there?," and "Will you promise to talk and tell us if you having any problems staying committed?"

The teacher and the parent become the embodiment of what is chosen, not imposed, and of the process of helping to make it happen, but they embody reality. They never relent or soften or dilute the original decision. Once the choice is made, it is the obligation of parents to uphold what was originally chosen. That builds commitment and responsibility.

EXAMPLES OF MI

Using the above five principles as guidelines, what are some of the ways parents can tap into the nine intelligences and bring them into play at home?

1. Linguistic Intelligence

Not only is this form of intelligence the most prized and used—Gardner after all explained his ideas in book form and you are reading one now—but it is the mother lode. However, what is often not acknowledged is that literacy—reading and writing—is a whole brain activity that involves all the many intelligences. Although visual, spatial, and even mathematical intelligence can enhance literacy, nothing very much can be accomplished and one cannot go very far without reading and writing. At a party or gathering you can get away with saying that you may have a block to math or science, but imagine the reaction if you claimed you could not read or write.

Parental and home acknowledgment of the centrality of literacy means minimally at least two activities: doing and modeling. Early on and for as long as you can get away with it, parents have to read to their children. The go-to-bed book should be a critical ritual in every home. It can be prolonged later by parents asking kids to take turns reading or by older kids reading to younger ones. Journaling, especially during a trip, can often become a family event when entries are shared at the end of the day to learn what each included and emphasized.

But parents also have to model the behavior they expect by being regular readers and writers themselves. Writing a letter together to grandparents, for example, instead of the weekly telephone call may be special. Even CEOs are now being urged to send handwritten notes of praise or congratulations to employees, and to put a real stamp on them and mail them to their homes.

One of the most powerful and least-known ways of supporting literacy is by enlisting the aid of some of the other multiple intelligences. Here are some examples of reinforcement:

- Spatial Intelligence—visual shapes of letters, pictures, and images. "Trace the shapes with your hand."
- Musical Intelligence—converting shapes into sounds. "What sounds do these letters or shapes make? Are they friendly or scary sounds?"
- Naturalist Intelligence—"Do these shapes resemble anything in nature? Do the sounds sound like any animals?"

- Bodily Intelligence—Visual and sound dimensions are like parts of the body that have to be reconnected to work together. The body is like a sentence or a thought. "Which shape or sound would you say is the brain, which one the heart, which one the legs?"
- Math Intelligence—"How do these letters and shapes and sounds organize themselves? In what order or sequence? Does the sentence add up? Anything missing that needs to be added?"
- Intrapersonal and Interpersonal Intelligence—"What do the sounds and shapes seem to be saying about feelings? About how one should react to the feelings of others? Are any of the words or sounds particularly strong feeling words as well as connecting words linking the feeling for others?"

In addition to supporting linguistic intelligence, each intelligence in turn can be separately described and the special strength and distinction of each one tapped by parents.

2. Bodily Intelligence

A wonderful example of the physicality of language on the one hand, and its capacity to stir physical reaction in turn on the other, is when, according to Thomas Armstrong (2003), a toddler discovers and uses the word "Up!" The magic of the word is that it has power; suddenly that one word causes Mommy to smile and offer her hands, Daddy to swoop her up in his arms for a kiss, and big brother to pick her up and take her where at least he thinks she wants to go. One physically related word is able to do the trick and influence the bodily movements of others. It also confirms the brain research that links language to bodily movement and reading to physicality in general. But clearly the major example is body language.

The key to reading the responses and attitudes of others through their body language is observation. Parents quickly can detect mood changes in their kids because, without fully realizing it, they have built up over time a series of emotional benchmarks. They can read their walks, how they hold their hands, their facial expressions, and so on, and they intuitively say, "What's wrong?" When the response brushes them off, they know they have hit pay dirt. They persist, "Something is off. Your body language gives you away. Tell us what is troubling you? Did something happen at school?" Often that releases, sometimes grudgingly, the truth.

Parents can teach their kids the generic skill of observation by practicing reading body language. Obviously teachers and members of the family are grist for the mill. The most powerful and insightful readers of body language are mimes. They not only can read the emotions of others, but also can perfectly replicate and feed them back to the original models. Kids also can be taught to do mime and thus amplify their repertoire of knowledge and discover the extent to which the body is an important part of intelligence. In the process, children become often more comfortable with their bodies and their special and often infallible form of communication.

3. Spatial Intelligence

Its range is enormous. It goes from tracing letters and even words in the air to designing graphs or spatial displays. I myself often have rendered fairly complicated contrasts between one period in time or condition of culture and another by creating a graphic matrix. It not only improves communication to an audience, but also pressures the clarity of the author. Such a chart also can act as a summary, as will appear at the end of this chapter.

The transformation of ideas, words, and thoughts into visual forms is a powerful teaching and learning tool. When working with kids at home, especially when they are having a rough time grasping a concept or mastering details, ask them to render their understanding in visual terms. Younger kids are more comfortable generally because they are more familiar with picture books, but older kids also can be led down the path of visual displays of their thinking. The advantage of spatial intelligence is that it moves ideas out of the brain, which wrongly is being used as a carrier or holder, to paper or blackboard where then the brain is free to do what it does best: comprehend. It is like the kid who is building something and working with tools. He carries around in one hand a tool that he had previously used but is not needed now and has lost that hand for the present task.

The famous admonition "A picture is worth a thousand words" is a tribute not only to art but also to visual communication. What is often called art appreciation in fact should also be the occasion for teaching visual intelligence. Parents need to stress that children and teenagers do not have to be artists to use visual thinking and rendering. For example, I am convinced that paper placemats were placed in restaurants so that engineers could turn them over and offer explanations in spatial drawings. In short, parents should stimulate spatial intelligence by teaching map reading, hanging blackboards in kids' rooms, suspending mobiles, putting the solar system on the ceiling, filling space in general with pictures. The problem with the current video generation is that their brand of visuality is too fast, sensational, manipulative, and technological to generate meaning. Traditional spatial thinking may in fact be needed more now than ever before.

4. Musical Intelligence

One does not have to be an accomplished musician to benefit from musical intelligence any more than one has to be a professional dancer to enjoy social dancing. Like linguistic intelligence, musical intelligence is wired in the brain and children are born with an immediate sensitivity to sound and rhythm. Many students are taught their ABCs to music; more advanced ones can learn and recite musically "Fifty Nifty States." Choral chanting is a special group musical art form that involves high school competition. Creative teachers sometimes shock their students by singing a text to and with them, or introducing current popular lyrics into a poetry class. Sometimes parents often do chores together by singing together or absorb time on a long car trip by singing songs.

But as in all the intelligences in MI, the key question is, What is this one able to do that the others cannot do as well or at all? Musical intelligence not only offers another voice and language, but also one that is universally shared by and that binds people together all over the world.

5. Math/Logical Intelligence

A strong linkage has been claimed between music and math. Many musicians have to master the math of music to use that common language to communicate with other musicians. However, many musicians often fail calculus. The other theory is that listening to music, especially Mozart, helps learn math. That argument is still going on, but the most fruitful approach for parents is to stress the value of math and numbers to better understand and master things. For example, many parents have a family budget, which in general terms can be shared with kids. Money and math are thus profound partners; they shape budgets and run checkbooks. Kids can be involved in not just deciding on where to go on a family vacation but in figuring out what different options will cost, and then using the spatial intelligence of a matrix to list all the options for everyone to see and discuss. This also involves planning for college and selecting certain savings plans. This should not be a mystery that shuts kids out. Math manages options.

A powerful blending of logical and organizational power with spatial intelligence occurs when kids are encouraged to make daily to-do lists, to use a student planner, to prepare outlines first for essays they have to write, and to use cluster or mind-set maps to display the rich world of their thinking. Typical well-constructed student planners include opening sections on time management and organizational skills. They also address the relationship between planning and notetaking, and studying and preparing for tests. In some homes, a master calendar is maintained, which brings together all the individual planning school entries of all kids and their many after-school activities plus all family and parental events. Without such organizational control mechanisms many modern families would be lost.

Without pressuring kids to become engineers, using math to comprehend and document activities or processes should sometimes be a subject of family discussions. A mechanical problem with any machine can be the subject of a larger discussion of quality control through quantitative means; ditto with the demographics of the census and actuarial tables of insurance companies and why it costs so much for kids under twenty-five (and what is so magical about twenty-five?) to secure car insurance. Certain ads directed at certain markets introduce kids to the math of marketing and segmentation and perhaps in the process make them more sales resistant or savvy. In short, the most important function of parents in the home is to inculcate the value of thinking quantitatively as a way of understanding and directing the world, whether or not it involves helping with trig or calculus. Parents do not in this case have to practice what they preach.

6. & 7. Intrapersonal and Interpersonal Intelligence

I have been in movie theaters where kids are so moved that at the end they applaud. The older ones do not. Increasingly and unfortunately the process of growing up in America often compels the suppression of our feelings. Even parents are sometimes emotionally subdued with their older kids, even abstaining from the affection of hugging and kissing. For quite a while men did not embrace each other; now it is more common.

The problem is that the youth culture often does not consider expressing emotions cool. To counter that, teachers and parents have to personalize what they talk about, select materials that are passionate, and attend plays and concerts that are moving. They can't allow their kids to go dead on them emotionally. Conversations have to develop habits of talking in terms of feelings, not just ideas or actions. Perhaps the most powerful ways parents can maintain the emotional intelligence of their kids is by community service or volunteer work. Many high schools require a set number of hours, but what I am talking about is the family doing community service as a family, whether it is through a religious organization or working the soup kitchen on Christmas Eve.

I have put together the two intelligences because it is a quid pro quo; the one needs the other for its authenticity. Helping is healing. It is also knowledge. My mother used to say, "What I don't know, I feel." Men as fathers need to cultivate their feminine side.

8. Naturalist Intelligence

Paradoxically, the natural world has become more and less important. Ecology, global warming, and water and fish shortages have dramatized the fragility of the planet earth. In contrast the world is becoming increasingly man-made, the most sensational examples of which are enormous cities and shopping malls. The Mall of America (aptly named?) in Minnesota even has become a tourist attraction; and Disney has made and tamed every animal, including ferocious ones like the Lion King, into charming talking and even singing characters. In the process nothing is made dangerous and kids are portrayed hopping from one wild adventure to another unscathed.

Parents need to strive for balance. They need to place emphasis on being responsible global citizens of ecology, recycling paper and tin cans, without invoking doomsday scenarios; but they also need to woo kids away from the illusions of always friendly nature into the more realistic world of biology. Fortunately, there are many excellent TV programs that should become family watching times together. Volunteering should include ecologically focused tasks such as cleaning up streams and rivers, as well as building humane shelters for dogs and cats. Although it smacks of packaging, there are a number of legitimate ecological tours to rainforests and deserts that families can take. The more your kids learn about the real world of nature, the better able they will be to ensure and sustain their survival and that of all the other creatures who cohabit this world with them.

9. Futuristic Intelligence

I have presumed to add this to Gardner's list for two reasons. First, I have found this kind of intelligence to be critically important in terms of problem solving, especially innovative problem solutions. Asking "what if" questions, thinking outside of the box, encouraging brainstorming, and so on, stimulates creative thinking and knowing. Second, given the exponential rate of change, anticipatory or proactive thinking, forecasting, and planning may well constitute our early warning and survival systems.

Parents can encourage this kind of intelligence by turning problems back on kids and asking them how they would solve the problem or address its future consequences. In school and at home, kids can be routinely encouraged to think creatively, to write scenarios of what might be, to prepare future legislation on dealing with an increasingly aging population, and so on. Reading and seeing science fiction films or video series are fine, but only if they are critically examined on the one hand, and students are invited to write alternative scenarios on the other. Otherwise it remains in the realm of technological sensationalism. In fact, high schools should offer courses on critical examination of contemporary media. Lacking such engagement in school or at home, students just become consumers, not critics, of their culture. In short, parents need to inculcate anticipatory habits of the mind in their kids if they are to reap the current and future benefits of anticipatory intelligence.

PUTTING GLASSER AND GARDNER TOGETHER

Glasser and Gardner have made it both tougher and easier to be effective parents. Glasser has indicated how high the stakes are, Gardner how complex the multiple paths are to student success. But they also have provided the tools and the intelligences to bring such success to both school and home. Indeed, one of the critical factors that nominates using both Glasser and Gardner is that they in fact straddle both areas. What each says to teachers they also say to parents, and vice versa. They bridge home and school and provide in the process a common language and culture of emotional and intellectual health. In fact by so doing they help to structure the common relationships between teachers and parents discussed earlier.

But for parents it is a daunting, complex, challenging, and never-ending task. In effect, every home has to have a family curriculum. Minimally, it has to include the psychological, the intellectual, and the family's belief system.

The last is created by each family; it is what it lives by. It may include not only familiar moral and religious values, but also the ideologies of ecology, helping the unfortunate, welcoming the stranger, and so on. That is how a family in fact puts itself together as a family. It is how a collective identity is made part of the identity of each member. It is what the family stands for as a family, supplemented by the contribution of each member's own identity.

If the major components of the family curriculum were to be rendered visually, it might take the following spatial form:

GUIDE	MODE	SCHOOL	HOME
Glasser	Choice Therapy	Self-Worth	Decisions
Gardner	MI	Multiply Smart	Well-Rounded
Parents	Family Curriculum	School Success	Happy and Caring Families

Blending, balancing, and believing—that is the multiple task of parents as teachers and homes as school. But the rewards always are multiple.

Part 4

PLANNING FOR CHOICES

It is inevitable: once choices proliferate, information and planning have to follow. Information serves to insure that the choices are informed. Planning looks ahead to the series of choices and to how each one chosen positions for the next and then the one after that. In this sense all educational planning is contingency planning. Increasingly, education is a chess game; every contemplated choice has to factor in and anticipate four or five moves ahead. In short, parents have to become master planners.

Schooling is now not a single but a multiple series of events. To the traditional checklist, parents now have to add and weigh technological capacity and technologically literate teachers, job and career prep, college preparedness, test pass rates, and so on. As if that were not enough, there are also the special and often different developmental patterns of each child. For those needing special attention, the list above would have to be expanded to include schools that offer a special ed program and an extended range of tutoring services and physical therapy. Even if special needs do not drive such choices, there are the normal chronological differences reflected in grade levels K–16.

What has made the current situation so different and more difficult for parents? How did the matter of choice become so complex in the first place? Most parents today did not experience in their growing up such an array of options. Not until the senior year were they required to decide where they were going and what they would be doing after graduation. However, education has evolved into almost a market economy. There are now multiple providers of educational services, and the services in turn are varied and segmented. How and why that has happened is a separate story that takes parents into the heart of the matter and the need for big picture planning.

But first it is necessary to stake out the future parameters of that big picture and to build confidence that in fact the future can be managed to support our planning. That in turn requires understanding how the future behaves.

WHY CAN'T THE FUTURE BEHAVE?

The future is often exasperating. It regularly behaves independently and even capriciously, as if it had a life of its own and can do whatever it wants. It is terribly elusive and even tricky, escaping the most ingenious calipers of strategic planning. Most frustrating of all, it has become increasingly so unpredictable that it has given greater credibility to science fiction and appears to have chosen that outrageous mode as the way it wishes to present itself to the world.

If the above characteristics were not so unsettling, and could be viewed with some distance and objectivity, all the complaints might make the future appear interesting. Indeed, as in many applications, the first step in higher-level problem solving is to value the difficulty of the problem, to perceive its opacity or enigmatic quality as not something created to torture but to task the problem solver. The more interesting the problem, the more rigorous the effort to solve it. The future as a problem is also layered—dense, multiple, angular. In other words, the solution, if there is one, will not come without an appropriate matching complexity of method. Finally, the future as a problem—as with difficult problems in general—has to be granted the autonomous power of being powerful and even destructive without being malicious. I suspect then, if we could only state our problems in these terms, our solutions might become more robust. In any case, a major source of difficulty in appreciating the future as an interesting problem is the number of questionable, obtuse, and even flippant assumptions and attitudes about the future that get in the way of its ambiguities. I have listed ten such obstacles below. The discussion that follows the list will directly and indirectly address all the items on the list in detail, but right now what is critical is to clear the field of error.

OBSTACLES OF PERCEPTION

"If your eyes are scratched, you see scratched."

Saul Bellow

1. No one can predict the future, so why bother?
2. We always have time to get around to the future. Just move it to next week's agenda.
3. The future is tabula rasa. It has no content other than what we give it.
4. In spite of all the talk about the end of the world, it never has ended.
5. The future will be enough like the past and the present to be familiar.
6. The bigger you are, the more immune you are to the vagaries of the future. Battleships can be hit but still sail on and hit back.
7. Things will be better in the future. In fact, one of the functions of the future is to give us time to catch up, improve, and change for the better.
8. The future will hold still while we change; and then the future can be updated.
9. The future generally has no constituency. The past does and so does the present; except for ad nauseam invocations by politicians dedicating something, valedictorians gazing off into the distance, and ecologists crying wolf, the future has few lobbyists.
10. The future is pretty straightforward. Although it is not a paper tiger, and although it is contradictory at times, even a little wild occasionally in its oscillations, for the most part the future is not complex.

SETTING THE RECORD STRAIGHT

No one who is serious about planning ever claims that the future can be predicted. Such a claim is usually a straw man set up to discourage, distort, or discredit long-term planning altogether. However, to say that one cannot predict the future is not to say that one can't understand it. Indeed, the argument here is that the future exhibits certain recurrent behaviors and operates under fairly regular patterns that, when comprehended, serve to legitimize forecasting. Specifically, attending to the future's ways has a number of other benefits. First, it anticipates and prepares for what may come and thus provides a more intelligent and flexible base for planning. It facilitates the creation of maps of the territory ahead so that change can be addressed and planned. It encourages supplementing participatory management with anticipatory management, which offers employees more direct access to identifying and having a say about their futures. Finally, most ambitiously and mysteriously of all, it promotes innovation as the incarnation of the future in the present.

BEHAVIORS OF THE FUTURE

If we take a long-term view of the future, examine its behaviors in the past, even in ancient times, and trace its evolution to the present, we will in effect be examining the history of the future. That developmental perspective is valuable because we are not generalizing about the behavior of the future only from modern times, although the isolation of the contemporary is valuable, but throughout time. Under such a perspective of history, what do we recurrently find?

1. The future is fast and sudden. It tends to arrive ahead of schedule. There is the sense that the change, once delivered, has always been there, so fast are things taken over. The future routinely generates accelerated returns, which in turn frequently subject our plans to diminishing returns. Why is the future so urgent? One reason is neglect. Ecology is a debt way past due, and it is pressing hard on survival and sustainability. Another reason is that the accelerators are tireless and automatic; technology now creates technology. Computer-assisted programs now design their own su-

perior programs. Nothing can escape the interconnectedness of globality; it surrounds and engulfs even provincial locales. IBM's small world is indeed that. Thus, one of the key behaviors of the future is speed. Whatever is to happen will occur rapidly, totally, and tenaciously. Note, we did not say without warning, for that leads to one of the other laws of the future.

2. The future sends warnings. The Greeks had the Delphic Oracle and the priests interpreting its omens. The Jews read dreams and developed the most extensive group of forecasters, the prophets. Christians employed revelations and the promise of the messiah. In all instances the key metaphor is the handwriting on the wall. The problem is we ignore or minimize the advance warnings. Indeed, it can be argued that the future exists in three versions: future stretch, strain, and shock. Initially, when the handwriting appears on the wall the adjustment and response are manageable; it is not inappropriate to invite people to stretch. But if that opportunity is foregone, then the future's law of escalated warnings takes hold. The next version is more difficult; the choices are fewer and grimmer as future strain dominates. If that opportunity is lost, then future shock enters the scene and crisis becomes the norm. The options are few and dreadful. A postscript: companies can be classified in terms of the degrees of commitment to the future. At least three states can be identified: future oriented, future directed, and future driven. Generally the last routinely finds it easy to embrace future stretch. The first holds out the longest and often falls into future shock. The middle child is always associated with strain.

3. The future is predictable, within limits. The future is a mixture of the known, the unknown, and the unknowable. It is predictable demographically. Population already here is biologically committed; and the actuarial tables of insurance companies have been making predictions for years. So have utilities based on the same data. So a significant portion of the future is known. The unknown portion of the future is not unknowable. Forecasters and futurists and strategic planners study, scan, and evaluate trends and megatrends. Worldwatch monitors global conditions and makes forecasts. Energy suppliers project demand and identify new sites

and sources of energy. Families invest in college funds and individuals in retirement plans, and companies make long-range plans. In other words, the unknown becomes more knowable and joins with the known to generate a fairly extensive base for comprehending the future. However, there is no negotiation possible with the unknowable future. That in fact is the way the future remains the future; it is its integrity. All presumption in the past—Prometheus, Adam, Faust, Frankenstein, and so on—is based on crossing that line and poaching on a divine preserve.

4. The future is always embryonic. It is always more than it seems—the proverbial tip of the iceberg. It is not unlike having one deer cross the road in front of you; at least one other will appear shortly. But it is dense, not easily "penetrable." Think of the development of the computer unfolding like an endless series of Chinese boxes. Once the future gives birth to technology, democracy, economic richness, ecological disturbance, and so on, there is no way of containing all its reverberations or determining where it will end. The future in its manifestations is seamless, internally interconnected. It resists linear sequential analysis; it is nonhierarchical. If it has a shape it is more like a river moving forward and around, changing the direction and speed of its flow. It is always a process, a system of processes, and its originality and brilliance lie in its design. It is more available to intuition, to the imagination of writers and poets, and to the scenarios of science fiction. In fact, science fiction generally has a better average in terms of forecasting than planners or futurists.

5. It is protean and mercurial, because its supreme law is that of transition. Unlike humans and organizations that seek perpetually the stability of a given order and regard transition as a temporary and unpleasant lull to be endured between one stable order and another that will appear, the future proclaims the permanence of transience. The future always announces itself as a transition that signals temporary disconnects or permanent dislocations. The false hope is that those transitions will be short and bearable, but they routinely have become longer and longer. Even when they appear to end, they give way not to a new stability but to another transition, and then to another. Indeed, the time condition of transition

is the present, just as the eternal present is the time of the future. The twenty-first century will be the century of transition as an archetypal norm.

6. The future is multiple. Its law will be that of moreness in everything. Here are some examples: Do more with less. More cross-training. More partnering. More alliances. More perspectives. More teaming. More learning. More diversity. More organizational and structural variety. More leadership opportunities and more leaders. More community and more isolation from community. More future-driven companies, and so on. In other words, the future potentially offers an overwhelming cornucopia.

7. The future is dualistic; it administers the slap and the caress simultaneously. It alternately offers a cornucopia of riches and severe limits to growth. There is a sting in its fruitful bower. Greed may unbalance all. The carrying capacity of everything may be compromised. The future embodies Nature's constraints and bounty; it speaks on behalf of centuries, not just decades, and it is capable of killing with kindness. Reading the constant doubleness of the future restores balance. It is the ecological check and balance system.

8. Most surprisingly and mystically of all, the future can be created. It can be hastened and lured into the present ahead of its time. The future is created whenever innovation comes into the world, whenever something new is discovered, unearthed, or brought into being. The future is incarnated by creativity, whether it is a light bulb, a gene, a new social theory, an educational breakthrough, a poem, or the birth of a creature. The fecundity of the future responds to the fecundity of innovation, and together they produce a second creation story. Indeed, one of the reasons the future moves with so much speed is that the pace and rage of innovation in this century has been incredible; and all indications are that it will be surpassed in the twenty-first century. The future, in short, is "Eureka!"

The future then is neither capricious nor elusive. It is swift but it warns. It is total but it offers the gradualization of future stretch, strain, and shock. It is unfamiliar and potentially discontinuous, but not to intuition and imagination. It is always circular, systemic in connections and flow, and theoretically without end. It is known and knowable up to a point: and then the gate is closed. It is ambiguously generous and stingy; it offers a caress and a slap. It speaks for Nature and for all limits to excess. It is increasingly multiple and compels a degree of moreness greater than any age before. Innovation incarnates the future in the present and gives it its body in this world. Innovation is the only incantation that draws what is to come into being and into the history of the future. Perhaps, finally, the question is not so much "Why can't the future behave?" but rather "Why can't we smarter about the way it behaves?" After all, that is where our kids will spend the bulk of their lives.

(12)

GUIDING EDUCATIONAL CHOICES

Perhaps the most unexpected direction that education has taken in the last decade is that of offering choices, and all indications are that the number and kind of choices will increase. Moreover, that applies not only to parents and their offspring, but also to all educators (teachers, administrators, educational trainers, etc.).

Of course, the traditional and historical options always have been and still are available: public, private, or parochial; but now there are many others: homeschooling, charter schools, cyberschools, and so on, and all sorts of variations on the original trinity of choices: private management–led public schools, magnet schools, alternative schools, performing arts or communications academies, hybrid or blended virtual and traditional schools, small academies within large high schools, high school/college schools, school-to-work schools, and so on.

The same variety also characterizes options being presented to educators as well. Internally, they are faced with options within options: curricula, technology, collaborative team learning, and so on. Externally, they may choose to leave the system altogether, to seek employment with a vendor that serves education, to shift to one of the other kinds of schools, or to aspire to administration. In fact, the choices they are offered and the ones they make are as important as what parents and kids choose as the school of their choice.

It may seem odd to join together parents, students, and educators in the same survey of educational options. It is not so for at least two reasons. First, the same forces that are impacting education to shape choices in the future are affecting all three. In fact, that is what determines the selection of driving forces affecting change and choice. To know the general and comprehensive guides the specifics. Second, it is critical for each constituency to know what the others value and why they choose what they choose. For example, if parents are contemplating choosing a charter school, they should know why the teachers and administrators of that school chose to work there. In turn, educators need to appreciate and understand what motivates parents now and is likely to affect their future family decisions. More so than at any time, education is an interlocking partnership.

THE PLANNING DYNAMICS

Consider the extent of the planning dynamic. Parents increasingly have to make decisions based on developmental stages, on the one hand, and on optimum positioning for the next choice, on the other. In effect they are contemplating and compiling a life educational plan which minimally covers a twenty-two-to-twenty-five-year span. It may begin with preschool, to be followed by K–3 devoted to homeschooling, and in turn may shift to traditional public or parochial or private school for the remainder of the elementary years. Middle school may be a charter school committed to implementing Gardner's multiple intelligences or project/inquiry learning. High school may be a cyberschool or hybrid blend of regular and virtual school to encourage socialization and participation in high school/college courses. States like Florida that are committed to K–16 planning now include college choice as well. To all this should be added that planning has to be individualized to be responsive to differences between kids in the same family as well as to different stages of their parents' lives.

The future is thus not an abstract idea to anyone who has or is planning to have kids. Children in fact embody the future and compel parents to be future focused. But no matter how much choice the future offers parents and students, it is neither simple nor does it always flow one way. The future requires knowledge, savvy, and smarts. The prize always goes to those who are proactive and are increasingly comfortable with living ahead of their time. Knowing what is ahead is like taking out an insurance policy on your children's educational life. Choice is the future of education, and decision making for all involved requires knowing the immediate and long-term options.

That is why the focus on the holistic future of education is so important. The operative perspective is to provide all the constituencies involved—parents, students, and educators—with the guidelines for choosing what each believes best serves their interests. Two factors make this venture special or unique: focusing on the long term and putting all the major players on the same team. Too often parents talk or listen only to parents, kids to kids, teachers to teachers, administrators to administrators. There is little or no cross-dialogue, no glue holding all together, no communication bridges; yet they are all involved in collectively shaping school environments and choice. Does it not make sense to bring all together to share the common focus of the future of American education and the future of American kids? Equally as important, does it not make sense to know as much as one can about the future of schooling and what is driving change in order to make the most informed choices?

⓵⓷ THE TEACHER-LED SCHOOL

If all the exciting and transforming initiatives, interventions, and outcomes that have occurred in corporate America in the last ten years were placed alongside all the exciting and transforming efforts of school reform, the contrast would be painful. To be sure, educators would protest comparing apples and oranges; but one need not choose between vision and profits. The most sensational recent example has been the launching of "K12," fronted by William Bennett, former Secretary of Education, but backed by the deep pockets of Mike Milken and his Knowledge University group of crusading investors. In addition, there are a number of for-profit companies that run schools. Other businesses have created and administered charter schools. They all are incorporated and pay taxes. Increasingly, it is no longer a question of whether or not businesses will enter education—they are already inside the gates—but which ones education wishes to partner with, as long as it has choices—and which business interventions it should embrace. In the opinion of many, education already has made the wrong choice by offering incentives to teachers for delivering the goods on state assessment tests. That is their job.

Incentives represent only one arrow in the extensive business quiver. Edison and other school management groups use some of the reengineering and empowering governance structures that seem to have eluded traditional schools. However, the critical question is, what sets business apart from education and sets it on a course that achieves goals of greater productivity, quality, customer satisfaction, and employee participation? Clearly, many characteristics present themselves as pivotal, but the key one is leadership. Moreover, what endows that subject with particular importance and even urgency is that the U.S. Department of Labor projects a significant shortage of principals and superintendents—some 20,000 by 2005.

This has led many school districts to scurry and develop rapid grow-your-own alternatives to standard certification and training. It also has led to the competitive business practice of offering hiring bonuses and even using recruiters and headhunters to lure existing administrators away or to find new ones. But as Arnold Jarger (2001) rightly notes, the problem is at the source. The search committees or headhunters are staffed and stocked with the same old people looking for the same old solutions. The applicant pool, in other words, is stagnant. Candidates who fit in are selected and hired; but because the pool essentially remains the same, they are not so much hired as recycled, just as the thinking and personnel of the search committees are. Then everyone is surprised that nothing changes and that nothing new emerges. But every once in a while desperation is the mother of invention.

The Los Angeles School District, the second largest in the country, spent more than three months looking for a new superintendent. Finally they did what many corporations routinely have done and what hardly any school districts have done: they hired someone outside the specific professional field. They brought in a former state governor, a decision which accurately reflects the increasingly political nature of that position. Saul Cooperman, former commissioner of education for New Jersey, supports the practice of going outside for talent: "Until we realize how insular we are as a profession . . . we will continue to lament the shortage of good applicants for our top positions. Meanwhile, a solution is before our very eyes" (Sobelly 2001).

What solutions are right in front of our collective eyes? There are at least two new tacks. New York City faced the same dilemma of not being able to find a superintendent. What saved the day was nothing less than a total reconfiguration of the job into two top positions: an educational leader and a business manager. The professionals who wanted to lead and the mangers who wanted to manage could now apply for what they really wanted to do, and they did.

What is instructive about both these decisions, and what apparently has been lost on the entire educational establishment, is that the job has changed. It is more political than ever before. It is also more difficult, perhaps even impossible, to be both an effective educator and a business manager at the same time. Typically one is good at one or the other or poor at both; yet these lessons and the creative responses on both coasts seem to have been totally ignored by all the school districts in between.

School districts for the most part are going about the same business of seeking and valuing the same kind of administrators who have been overwhelmed for years. There is no recognition that education has hit a leadership brick wall. Instead of seeking creative solutions, the knee-jerk reflex is to do the same thing all over again. There does not appear to be any interest in invoking the principle of operation leapfrog—while we are catching up let us also try to get ahead and think outside the nine dots.

Most disturbing of all, a solid argument can be made—in fact, has been made—that the current body of educational administrators for the most part has failed to accomplish school reform. Many teachers in fact have suggested that they are part of the problem rather than the solution. That is not totally surprising. Deming (1993) claimed that 85 percent of all problems were the fault of managers; yet there is little sign of examining the current job descriptions of administrators and developing alternative training formats that are a bit more experimental and daring than tweaking a few courses. One of the most lasting principles of Hammer and Champy (1993) in their work on reengineering organizations and reengineering managers is that nothing is sacred. Cherished assumptions must be questioned and sacred cows challenged. There may be a better model of educational leadership than the one we have that currently dominates present systems. The model proposed here—the second solution before our eyes—is that of the teacher leader and of the teacher-led school.

Is it really not an outlandish idea after all? Almost all principals and superintendents were originally teachers. To be sure, the average amount of time since they were last in the classroom, sadly, is nine years. It would be interesting to know how many were good teachers, what led them to leave, and how their teaching style and performance affected their leadership style and expectations. Not unlike the doctoral candidate whose bibliography stopped with the date of his dissertation, many principals often reveal their basic teaching approach when they lecture teachers on how and what to teach, even though many have not been in the classroom for many years. In any case, we are not talking about an exotic or strange import to the system. What then would be different from the standard step of teachers becoming administrators?

At least ten things would change:

1. Teachers would become leaders without becoming certified administrators.
2. They would remain in the classroom.
3. There would be many learning leaders, who collectively would replace principals.
4. The business side of the house would be taken care of by business managers. Indeed, many of these functions can be outsourced.
5. Not all teachers would become learning leaders. The number needed would be determined by the nature of the learning design and economic resources.
6. The approval of regular teachers would be required for those who applied to be learning leaders.
7. They would be paid more.
8. They would serve three-year renewable terms.
9. They are removable and renewable by a majority vote of teachers in the unit.
10. They chair a committee of parents.

How would it work? There could be a number of configurations, but there are certain common structures that would have to be there to preserve the integrity of the solution. Learning leaders would assume responsibility for administering learning on grade or subject matter levels.

They would take the lead in facilitating collaborative lesson and pupil review. Each administrative unit would run its own house and never exceed one hundred students. Decisions would take place at the basic unit level. Unlike site-based management, decisions would not take the form of recommendations presented to the principal for review and decision. In other words, the decision-making process would be always proximate to instruction. A council of learning leaders would generate broad policies, goals, standards, professional development activities, and future plans. Coordination would take place, but not standardization, between different schools in the district.

The model of the learning leader already exists to some extent. It is functioning effectively in certain schools with empowering principals who have recognized that the only way to turn schools around is to use and support the teachers who have to do the leading. Without their cooperation and collaboration nothing really happens or lasts.

Of course, it happens regularly and comprehensively in business and probably is more responsible than any single factor for the steady increase in profitability and productivity nationally and globally. Teaming and cross-training have become norms. In some plants, task teams have proven that people productivity easily matches and even exceeds technological productivity. Above all, these new knowledge workers have increasingly made the roles of managers and engineers marginal, even superfluous. They determine schedules, maintain quality, ensure customer satisfaction, find innovative shortcuts, hire future employees, and enjoy profit and gain sharing. In short, given the national trends of empowerment throughout the country, even in government, education finds itself generally isolated or playing the role of catch-up. Typically, they have gone the route of the fast and dirty by seizing upon financial incentives to lure teachers out of the classroom to become administrators. However, it will not work for a number of reasons.

Incentives are bonuses, not permanent increases in base salary. Districts in fact often use dollars taken out of the pot reserved for salary increases. Teachers know that once the problem is solved or fails to be, the incentives will disappear. Besides, money generally has failed to motivate innovation. Bribery does not stir aspiration; it is a mismatch; and most serious of all, it is a half passed off as a whole. It is not meaningful to extract one element from a total reconfiguration of reinforcing factors and expect it to function as an effective substitute for all the others. The entire process has to be overhauled if the desired outcome is to be cumulative and integrated.

Nothing shows the ignorance and desperation of education more than the recent cynicism of financial incentives to buy change and school reform. It won't work because it is a shortcut and a cheap shot. It is manipulative, and that alone will fail not only to buy the aspiration or commitment of teachers (and parents), but also create more alienation and even invite sabotage. Only if education recognizes that it is at a crossroads and that its future depends on total review of its structure, operating principles, and the need to empower teachers will genuine change come about. The notion of teacher-led schools is only one of many possible new developments, but it also has a history of success in business.

The notion of learning leaders first emerged in the works of Robert K. Greenleaf and Clifford Pinchot, who advocated the kind of distributed leadership that teacher-led schools would happily endorse. Both authors sought to liberate leadership from the monopolistic hold of CEOs and senior management. They argued that leadership should be available to everyone and in fact be written into every job description. Distributed leadership moved many organizations away from the inhibiting ego cult of the one savior leader, tapped the natural abilities and innovative ideas of countless employees, and emphasized the organization as a leader in the industry. One of Greenleaf's favorite Taoist proverbs was that when leaders are successful the people say "We did it ourselves."

However, teacher-led schools will not come about easily or quickly. There are many obstacles, but three have the capacity to wreck the new venture before it really starts. Sadly, the biggest obstacle is teachers themselves. They are brainwashed. They are dependent. They are taught in colleges of education to obediently follow the chain of command. The suggestion even has been made that because it is a largely female teaching work force, and principals and superintendents are largely dominated by men, there is gender dependency as well. But the insidious problem is that often there is a love-hate relationship between teachers and administrators. The latter are often regarded as necessary evils, and even when they are demonstrably more evil than necessary, even then the prospect of their not being there as the final decision makers strikes terror into the hearts of teachers. The hunger for a final arbiter makes administrators indispensable. Who will deal with angry parents? Who will discipline that child? Who will interpret policy and explain all the dos and don'ts of the rules and regs? Who will make the final decisions? And so on and so on.

The second major obstacle is that in many cases principals have done an effective job of ensuring their indispensability. Like the proverbial Victorian husband who takes over the management of a wife from the proverbial tyrannical father, principals continue the culture of teacher dependency from colleges of education; and lest it slip away from them, they determine who gets hired and what is offered as professional development. In a number of businesses, employee universities have been set up with curricula determined by employees and even taught by many of them. Obviously, the biggest resistance will come from principals themselves, who are not about to give up their positions to teachers. Their professional associations will do everything they can to discredit and prevent that from occurring. Sadly, even some teachers' unions may not support this new kind of empowerment. They do not wish to antagonize educational administrators with whom they have maintained a cozy negotiating relationship. Then, too, teacher leadership is too new, and too limited in numbers and scope, and it has yet to be fully evaluated. Thus, although at this point it is more of a rallying point than a mainstream movement, parents may wish to monitor its progress and impact carefully, because its advocates tend to be parent-centered.

Finally, there is the reluctance, if not outright opposition, of the remaining establishment players: school boards, colleges of education, state departments of education, PTAs, and so on. School boards are in the accountability game; they want to deal with one person whom they can boss around or fire. Professors of education would not know how to train teacher leaders; they immediately would push them into programs for training administrators. Worst of all, they might have to talk to the business faculty, whom they have snubbed and sniped at for years, and who inhabit a totally different building, which they have never visited. The state boards of education want to keep their lives simple and uncomplicated. They do not want to enter a new no-man's-land and develop new credentialing standards that straddle teachers and administrators. Parents would wring their hands and worry rightly about their children being pawns in this latest school reform and opt for the status quo, and so it would go.

At this point, with so many forces arrayed against it, who is for it? Probably, only a minority of most of the groups mentioned here are: teachers, principals, some school boards, professors of education, parents, and so on, but they are not aware of each other. They don't know that they exist as potential fellow partners. There is no forum for exchange, and even if they did know about each other, minority solutions are always suspect. The demand is that it be an all-or-nothing affair. Everybody has to change or nobody should. In fact, that is symptomatically the response and sign of a monolith. One cannot fight the system because it is intact, big, and impervious. Like an impregnable fortress it has survived decades of attack and still requires uniformity and standardization.

Some claim that competition resulting from school choice will force education to change. Maybe, but that is a long way off, if it ever occurs. Besides, when education is threatened it becomes defensive. It then always trots out its standard rhetoric of protecting our children, and invokes the prospect of children being used as guinea pigs. It intimidates parents into staying with the status quo and not rocking the boat, and protective parents and conservative school boards are regularly swayed.

In any case, the strategy is not to play the game of all-or-nothing and seek to persuade the system to change totally. Rather, the focus has to be on forming alliances and gathering sufficient support to be an experimental or pilot program. In short, the key is to remain a minority movement. Learning Leaders in Teacher-Led schools have to go about the business of establishing a new minority standard of best practices quietly and persuasively, without fanfare, and certainly without martyrdom. Learning leaders have to build an alternative structure for administration and instruction. If they succeed in building a better mousetrap, then and only then will others beat a path to their doors, and all will acknowledge that they did it themselves.

14

FIVE FUTURE MODELS OF
SCHOOL LEADERSHIP

Not unexpectedly, the focus on school reform has resulted in challenging and scattering a number of sacred assumptions. Uncertainty alone may make it even more difficult to attract outstanding candidates to fill the projected shortages of teachers and principals. Perhaps nothing more dramatizes the fluid nature of the current environment than the number of options being discussed for educational administration. Indeed, for the first time, perhaps, teachers as teachers (not as administrators) are being offered a distinct option as part of the management mix.

Generally speaking, there are at least five major leadership models that are discernible. (All currently coexist, sometimes even in the same school district.) The first two are based on the traditional model of the principal with variations. One seeks an enlargement of the principal's role; the other argues for reducing the range of the role, but not with any sacrifice of centrality or authority. The third or middle position advocates distributed, not singular, leadership. It follows a multiple management model in which various individuals, more or less equals, singly, collectively, and collaboratively administer the school. The fourth and fifth options, like the first two, are also variations on each other and curiously exhibit the same emphasis on arguing for more or less. But what is dramatic about these last two options is the emphasis on teachers as administrators, while remaining teachers. These last two options are part of the larger pattern, in which teachers are being asked or offered to do more than teach. In the fourth version teachers work together with the principal to lead and manage the school. This arrangement basically represents a partnership of equal unequals. It also can be designated a version of the distributed model. Fifth and finally, the most radical version is that of teacher leader, capable of functioning without any principal at all. This also establishes for the first time the model of a teacher-led school and in some states a teacher-owned school. Each of the five options has its own advocates and needs to be addressed separately and specifically.

1. LEADERSHIP EXPANDED

Those championing expanding the role of the principal argue that such is required to ensure school reform. The principal has to be the supreme instructional leader. The claim is that this role is the key to improving school performance and accountability. However, the problem is that every administrator is limited in the range of his expert subject matter. The more the principal expands his instructional leadership, the more he crosses over into areas beyond his knowledge; and it is at those points that teachers may withdraw and question whether he knows what he is talking about. In part this dilemma has led to advocacy for distributed leadership, which is really distributed subject matter competencies. The principal has to stop short of claiming generic subject matter competence and instead share the leadership of the whole in a distributed fashion with those who hold the various competencies.

2. LEADERSHIP CONTRACTED

The second model calls for principals to do less. The plate is already too full: the supervisory requirements for managing special education; Title IX, which has doubled athletic programs with the addition of girls' sports; and the new safety and security regulations mandated by the federal and/or state governments. Indeed, many worry that the job of the principalship will be defined in such a way that few will want the job, or even fewer may be effective in it. Particularly sad is the number of principals who exhibit the classic hubris of displaying an excessive pride in their martyred exhaustion. In other words, if the assumptions about the range and the focus of the principalship are not challenged, all the attention being given to the principalship will remain unrelated to the larger issue of school reform, and we will have lost the opportunity to attract, train, and retain the new principals of the twenty-first century.

3. LEADERSHIP DISTRIBUTED

A number of concerns led to the development of distributed leadership. First, the increasing complexity and verticality of large school systems was distancing employees from the decision-making process. That was particularly lamentable because they had a great deal to contribute. Indeed, there appeared to be a strong link between participatory decision making and innovation. In effect then a double gain was being offered.

Second, leaders should not believe that they are indispensable and enjoy a monopoly of leadership. Indeed, the litmus test of the true leader is his regular transfer of leadership from the CEO to the organization. Leadership is not in fact the sole prerogative of the CEO or the principal. Rather, it is available to everyone in the organization. Indeed, some institutions write it into employee job descriptions.

Third, distributed leadership reinforces the role of the leader in developing everyone's potential. That requires leveling the vertical to the horizontal so that the collective and collaborative task of administering the school is diffused across the board. Subject matter competence is left in the hands of those who already possess it. Distributed leadership is not a recasting of committees where teachers make recommendations to the almighty vertical god, but a genuinely horizontal and participatory collaborative. However, the key is the willingness of the principal to be less than the total authority, to share not just responsibility but also power, and to endow each teacher with a participatory role in decision making.

Distributed leadership is gradually taking hold. In the Montgomery County school district in Maryland, teachers have been appointed to serve as instructional improvement leaders; in Rochester they are called consultant teachers. In either case they now do what principals did or were supposed to do: stir instructional development by stimulating teacher development. The strength of this arrangement is that it avoids the problem of leadership and of subject matter mismatch.

Under the aegis of distributed leadership, an organization increasingly becomes cooperative, collective, and collaborative. The vertical pyramid is leveled horizontally. Hopefully, what emerges over time is an innovative and futuristic school system that is a leader in the field. In addition, distributed leadership in effect has forced to the forefront questions that up until now have not even been posed before: Who shall lead? What shall be the leadership configurations of the future? The increased burdens imposed on the principalship, the bifurcated structures of districts that force management and academics to exist and function as parts of, and even at odds with each other, and the general incapacity of a number of current administrators to achieve real proximity to and leverage on teacher development and student achievement as a unified and reciprocal focus, have created a vacuum, which teachers in large part and for the first time alone are filling.

4. LEADERSHIP PARTNERED

Curiously, the fourth model derives its impetus and strength from the intellectual limitations on one leader being able to see 360 degrees and to command comprehensive subject matter competence. The principal of McCosh School in Chicago, Barbara Watkins, shares leadership with a teacher team that collectively runs the school. In this case, Watkins is not even first among equals on the team. In fact, the group says, "We're all leaders." The principal's role is more external and noninvasive. Basically, she prods and stimulates the administrative team to make informed and optimum decisions. She functions as the voice of parents and the community, and shares business perceptions. She is also a political analyst, making them aware of the internal realities of the district, the priorities of the superintendent and the school board, the concerns and constraints of the city and state legislatures, and the demands upon her and the assurances she has to give when she signs documents of accountability. Finally—and here is where the issue of instructional leadership joins the case—she serves as an advocate for a triangle linkage: teacher development, student achievement, and subject matter best practices. Significantly, many of the teachers themselves direct teacher development workshops.

All four models surveyed preserve the principalship to a greater or lesser degree:

1. The principal needs to do more, particularly in providing instructional leadership. Therefore, let us help him expand his role as an academic leader.
2. The principal needs to do less, especially if he is to provide instructional leadership. Therefore, let us find ways to relieve him of his business and managerial duties.
3. But in both cases the principal needs to establish subject matter credibility. Therefore, we need to develop a new definition of subject matter competence for the principal: leadership content knowledge or leadership literacy.
4. The principalship needs to be extended horizontally so that it is distributed rather than concentrated. That also will solve the problem of the limited range of subject matter competence and acceptance.

Finally, trust can guide benign abandonment: a team of teachers can be empowered to run the school. The principal moves from the center to the periphery. Watkins becomes a broker, an internal consultant, an executive team coach. She has become a guide on the side rather than a star on the stage.

Throughout, preserving the principalship in one form or other is still the focus. But is there a next step where all these models in fact may be leading us to? The solution of maintaining principals may be the problem—the obstacle to the next step. Implicit in the Chicago leadership partnership is still another alternative model: that of the teacher leader, who may have the capacity to be even superior to the conventional single principal in all its variations.

5. TEACHER-LED SCHOOLS

Teacher-led schools are mostly to be found among charter schools, such as those belonging to the cooperative of Ed/Visions in Minnesota. It existed earlier as the vision or metaphor of a number of educational researchers who believed if education would embrace teacher leadership as a meaningful option, it would do much to reposition education in the twenty-first century. To appreciate its difference as a model from the others, it may be helpful to list its main governance distinctions:

1. Teachers alone provide educational leadership. There are no principals.
2. They remain teachers in the classroom.
3. They are not identified as administrators and thus do not require state or district certification.
4. They are learning leaders, each in charge of a team responsible for a cohort of no more than 100 students. Scale provides coherence and community; small is always better than big. The number of learning leaders needed would be determined by the population and its operating structure.
5. Like the Cohosh partnership, each learning leader would be assisted by a collaborative team of teachers, tutors, techies, parents, and so on, who would service the cohort.
6. The business side of the house would be handled by a business manager, whose task it would be to facilitate educational goals and not create financial fiefdoms of bureaucratic impotence. Some functions would be outsourced.
7. Cost controls would be a collective team responsibility. Budgets may not be exceeded. Any surpluses remain with the team and may be carried over to the next operating year.
8. Evaluation of students would take the form of 360-degree assessments that would factor in high-stakes testing but not be the only or even primary source of evaluation.
9. Appointment of learning leaders requires team teacher approval. They serve three-year renewable terms. They are paid at least 30 percent more than the highest-paid teacher. New members of the learning team are hired and fired by the team.

10. Learning leaders are removable or renewable by a majority of the members of the team.

11. Learning leaders of all cohorts constitute the Learning Leader Council to establish schoolwide goals, priorities, policies, and procedures. Elected reps from this group make up the districtwide council.

12. Finally, and most important of all, the mission of each learning team is to provide for the integration of Administration, Instruction, and Measurement (AIM) in the classroom. That way administration and measurement are intimate and proximate to instruction, feedback is constant and immediate, diagnostics and interventions follow on each other's heels, and students centered by 360-degree assessments and teachers by a similar holistic structure are involved in a seamless and transparent process.

Would it work? It already has. In effect it is the next step in the evolution of delivering distributed collaborative education. Leadership would be transferred directly to the classroom and to teachers. No elaborate intermediary structure or roles would be needed, because they would have been internalized within a new collaborative unit, which simultaneously administers, teaches, and measures the effectiveness of student achievement.

Will it be adopted by others? Perhaps as a last resort. If enough are persuaded that tinkering with the first two models of the principalship takes care of the problem, that will remain the dominant solution. A number may hearken to Elmore's distributed leadership, and a lesser number will follow the Chicago model. Sadly, many teachers for the most part will probably not support teacher leadership; probably only about 5–10 percent will. The prospect of not having a paternal figure as the principal strikes terror in their hearts. Nor would the unions, which one might believe would happily embrace the cause, do so. They have developed a number of relationships with the existing administrative hierarchies that are too comfortable for them to become adventurous. Even school boards that are accustomed to the clarity of finding fault with administrators would not be happy to confront a host of teacher leaders. Obviously, the various associations of professional administrators will resist the idea of teacher leaders to the death.

So what is the upshot? Are we tilting at windmills? The argument comes down to this: administrative partnerships, with or without principals, should represent and be perceived as a respectable minority option for both teachers and principals. As such, there is the need to provide the separate visibility and viability of an alternative. Such an option needs to be held up by serious advocates of school reform to the new teachers and administrators who will be filling current and future vacancies. There is even the possibility of attracting professionals who ordinarily might not consider entering education. Specifically, such alternatives may attract administrative candidates open to partnering and distributed leadership, and teachers who may be receptive to becoming teacher leaders. Equally as important, these alternatives must be put before colleges and professors of education so that they might begin to prepare teachers for being leaders without becoming administrators, and administrators for being principals without being lone rangers. Above all, we have to preserve the prospect that we may be describing a new future norm and that the current minority position may in fact become a dominant one. If in fact that occurs then the current discussion follows the dynamics of leapfrogging—while we are catching up let us also seek to get ahead. The future houses all the alternatives. We just have to take the next step.

(15)

THE EDUCATION PLANNING CLEARINGHOUSE

Parents need help to undertake the kind of planning needed to guide and optimize the educational and career future of their kids. Consider the complexities before them: choices of kinds of schools, curricula, teachers, involving a span of at least ten to fifteen years; positioning them to pass annual test hurdles; the possible need for outside supplemental tutoring, and so on. That does not include having the financial means to support kids growing up as well as sustaining a college fund; nor does it factor in parental factors at all: changing or losing jobs, having to relocate, going back to school, and so on. The prospect of educational planning may be even more formidable than financial planning, for which there are professionals available for hire.

Who can help parents in this daunting task? To be sure, some parents hire specialists to assist with college selection and admissions. Others secure advice early on from investment counselors in setting up college fund savings accounts. A number of states have set up on behalf of their residents a tuition savings plan focused on attending a state university. Tuition is frozen at the date of enrollment, modest interest is provided, and the total saved can be applied to a private college or returned in a lump sum to parents. However, no comparable public effort is provided to parents who need guidance to thread their way through the increasingly labyrinthine maze of educational planning.

Clearly, what is needed is for education itself to provide the service. It already has the staff of competent counselors available. Extra or specialized help can be acquired on a part-time or outsourced basis. As part of supervisory licensure, administrators are introduced to various planning systems and of course many already have had a number of years of planning experience. Besides, they are familiar with the complex and often bureaucratic workings inside the system. Retired SCORE volunteers could also be tapped, and some parents could be trained minimally to provide assistance to planning counselors.

If the service is so badly needed, and the means to deliver it are already there, why has it not happened? For three reasons:

1. The High Road Not Taken

Many school districts have bad-mouthed most if not all of the alternatives to traditional public schools, especially charter schools and cyberschools. In addition, they have publicly bewailed the damaging social isolation of homeschooling. Threatened by the increasing competition of school choice, administrators and teachers often have struck out, sometimes joined by unions, to undermine educational alternatives. In short, providing parents and students with a public planning service that would include all choices evidently requires such an extraordinary act of educational leadership to take the high road that few will elect to do it in the current competitive climate of holding on to what you have and hunkering down for the future.

2. Catching Up with the Present

So much change has beset education itself that it devotes more of its time to catching up with the present than to looking ahead. For example, as testing and measurement have come to the fore and dominated data tracking systems, to stay current and on top of things many school districts have hired assessment administrators. These are new jobs that a few years ago did not even exist. They in turn may require a technical support staff, which taxes resources. Then, too, many school districts have created and staffed Offices of School Choice to manage the often intense process of preferential school and teacher choices. The explanation then for the absence of public planning assistance is that schools have just not caught up with a pressing need because it is oriented to the future and because it involves parents.

3. No Planning Model Exists
The existence of enabling mechanisms often invites initiative. Conversely, its lack discourages action. The fact is that no district has developed a parents planning model, and because in addition that need has not achieved high market visibility, no commercial development seems likely in the immediate future. So in anticipatory fashion, we are at the beginning of the learning curve, and for better or worse the design of the model is in our hands.

THE EDUCATIONAL CLEARINGHOUSE

Structure

The comprehensive control, direction, and planning of educational choice become the facilitating responsibility of the central administration of the entire school district. In effect, the planning role would expand the mission commitment of the district. The central office would function as a Clearinghouse for parents and kids. Instead of viewing different educational choices as competing and rating them as superior or inferior, all would be perceived as equally valid options. The final value would be determined by parents as part of a projected series of match-ups between choices available and needs of kids.

Range

The one-stop planning service would be an optional service provided to families who wish to make use of district assistance in exploring and planning ahead for the future education of their offspring. Although the service may occur from any age forward, the Clearinghouse is longitudinally total. It ranges from pre-K to college selection and completion.

Parents may in fact enroll their kids prior to or at birth. Indeed, just as parents, grandparents, or relatives create and contribute to a college fund for newborns, so infants may be registered in the Clearinghouse and deposits made for the service. In fact, one of the services provided is a list of college planning arrangements available to parents and other interested parties.

Costs

Additional staff or redeployment of existing staff will be required. Given the characteristic compulsion of administrative expansion, a new administrator in charge of the Clearinghouse will have to be appointed. Even training of citizen and parent volunteers will involve workshop expenses. In short, it is simple arithmetic: adding a service adds costs, and left unaddressed this serves as a further obstacle to implementation.

Costs have to be shared at least initially three ways: the district has to secure additional budgetary support from the school board; the local PTAs, many of which already have set up community educational foundations, have to make funding of the Clearinghouse a high priority; and parents using the service as an option have to pay a planning fee based on a sliding scale tied to income. Even if a school district or PTA secured a planning grant, eventually the cost of sustaining the operation would become a local matter.

Staff

The Clearinghouse would be staffed by educational planning counselors. Although all would have generic competence and range, there would be minimally four specialist groups: pre-K and elementary, middle school, high school, and college. In addition, there would be general counselors with specialized knowledge of charter schools and cyberschools and the complexities of homeschooling. Finally, the Clearinghouse center would be totally wired. Computer and Internet website access would be featured to encourage independent pre- and post-planning exercises by parents and kids. Indeed, the planning process itself is conceived as an increasingly do-it-yourself total family activity. The role of Clearinghouse staff is to help launch and orient families to the process, provide midpoint corrections and amplifications, and lastly, jointly review final plans and choices. In short, the process is intentionally designed to involve increasing participation and ownership from parents and kids to the point where final choices are always familial and not of those of the Clearinghouse or its staff.

THE PLANNING MODEL AND PROCESS

Although different models can be developed, a basic and comprehensive one is that of a longitudinal road map accompanied by rules of the road. Ideally set up as a board game that would engage kids, it also would be available in both a hard copy and computerized form. The advantage of the latter is that it could easily invite and sustain multiple simulations of choices along the planning route, as well as serving as a retrievable document for review or final printing. Above all, it easily facilitates tracking and monitoring along the way and last-minute changes, additions, and corrections.

To a large extent the use of a road map taps into the power and process of Lifelines. This staple workshop exercise invites retrospect and prospect, looking back and looking ahead. Individuals draw a lifeline identifying in the process all the key branch points they encountered; what choices were available to them; what choices they made; and what were the impacts of those choices not only on immediate events but on choices available to them later. In the process, the role of positioning assumes significant importance, because each choice is perceived as making possible or impossible certain other choices. In addition, the road less traveled by, and often hence not chosen, may be invested with greater significance associated with its greater risk. In short, because of its directional and often sobering value, the Lifelines exercise is given to all parents to complete; and it is recommended that it be shared with their kids.

The road map will be a busy one. Minimally, it will include all the chronological branch points of school choice, even backing up to before kindergarten and extending beyond high school. It also can accommodate through different symbols curricula choices, especially those like service learning, which involves choices of kinds of community service. Obviously, it will now have to include all state-mandated testing subjects and grades, as well as later AP options. It would be a good idea also to factor in vacation times and trips, especially if they have or serve an educational dimension. Teenagers in particular may wish to contemplate afterschool or summer jobs or volunteer assignments, especially those that they may involve travel abroad.

If there are siblings, planning also should be shared and ultimately coalesced into a cumulative family plan because both time and funds may be limited. That way each kid has his or her own plan, but by making it part of an overall collaborative plan it may stand a better chance of happening. It also would insure the centrality and equity of the family unit, which are always the double balancing act sustained by parents.

What will be the effect of such a planning initiative? Initially, kids may be bewildered and unfocused, but gradually, especially if it is presented as a board or computer game, their mind-set will be enlarged. Above all, it will serve appropriately as a different but complementary learning experience to their other school learning experiences, and introduce them to the critical process of fusing life and learning planning seamlessly and with the protection of first thinking about it on paper before acting on it.

FAMILY- RATHER THAN SCHOOL-CENTERED

In this proposed configuration, public education would regain its leadership role of servicing all. Every central office would become an advocate not of different versions of education, but of the different developmental needs of students. To allow the current infighting and competition to drain energy and resources on the one hand, and to cast families and students adrift in a sea of confusing choices and mandated tests on the other, cries out for commonsense leadership. If it is not forthcoming from educators, parents may have to step forth and save the day. Indeed, increasingly parental leadership is becoming not only the object but also the agent of school reform.

16

TEACHER–PARENT PARTNERSHIPS

The problem with lip service is that it often sanctions paralysis. The problem with tokenism is the conclusion that the status quo is as much as can be done or as far as one can go. For example, there is total agreement about the importance of parental involvement. Some even claim it matches instruction in impact. All the research is uniformly confirming and conclusive. However, other than some electronic communications upgrades and teacher and administrative cheerleading, little has really been done to tap parental resources for specific instructional goals, and nothing of substance has been done to link teacher involvement with parental involvement.

What makes that sin of omission so glaring is that it occurs at a time when teachers and schools need all the help they can get to ratchet up student performance. Instead, we appear to be turning our collective backs on a resource that not only could spell the difference now, but also offer key future support. Why? On the multiple answers to that question hang a significant challenge to educators.

There are at least three reasons why educators have not moved aggressively forward on implementing parental involvement plans: time, roles, and variability.

1. TIME

Teachers and administrators find their present plates already full and even overflowing. Many teachers do not even have the time for grade level or subject matter meetings; and if they had to choose between meeting with parents and with their colleagues, they would choose the latter, although all educators admit that in an ideal world every teacher has two significant others: other teachers and parents.

2. ROLES

Educators are reluctant to assume the role of family or marital counselors or social workers. They have enough trouble teaching their kids. Any educator who has been exposed to parents knows how often and how much some parents seek to explore their family situation in detail, and in the process ask both educators and the school to take on or help with their particular dysfunctional situation. Teachers draw the line and shut off.

3. VARIABILITY

Parental variables are incredibly diverse: the extent of their education, values, economic circumstances, nationality, availability, religious affiliation, educational and career expectations for themselves and their kids, and so on. It is neither possible nor would it be productive to develop a one-size-fits-all approach. Instead, it would have to be doubly individualized to reflect the learning situation of each student and then to match that with the special situation of each set of parents or single parent.

Given the above obstacles, it is not surprising that parental involvement remains a distant, vague, and hoped-for add-on, but has not generally been made an integrated part of instruction, administration, or evaluation. But what if enlightenment (the research) and desperation (home support of performance) converged and made parent involvement a high enough priority to compel implementation? What would such a program look like?

Minimally a number of components would have to be present and certain preconditions would have to be made explicit.

I. RANGE

The extent of parental involvement would be defined. The following chart displays the range:

EXTENT	ROLE
Minimum	Review
Intermediate	Supervision
Maximum	Involvement
Optimum	Partnership

The roles are not statically fixed once and for all time. In most cases, they can be progressive. Also other variables would be involved: choices would vary with changing circumstances, the stages of the kids involved, the degree of commitment at any given time, etc.

2. BOUNDARIES

Exchanges would be limited to educational matters only. The school would provide a list of public, private, and religious counselors for in-depth marital and family discussions.

3. TRAINING

Two kinds of parent workshops would be provided. First, the school or district would provide generic parent-school involvement training for parents. That would include student success factors, current research findings, and what constitutes a supportive home atmosphere and environment for learning. It also would include limiting TV watching time to no more than two hours per day, parental review of homework, and regular home communications about school. Given prescribed areas, parents would routinely provide feedback. Second, teachers would provide workshops on grade level and subject matter expectations and outcomes. These would be not only spelled out in detail, but also in terms of specific parental support and direct involvement.

4. LEARNING AGREEMENTS AND ARRANGEMENTS

Whether such arrangements take the form of parental learning contracts, teachers must in effect routinely develop two sets of lesson plans. The first is the standard one for daily and weekly instruction; the second is the lesson plan for the teacher's instructional partner. The two should be developed together in order to be in synch. The learning partnership goals can range from basic skills acquisition and testing to advanced assignments. Most importantly, the achievement of the parental goals is to be perceived as pivotal. The teacher has to be able to count on the specifics being accomplished by the time she arrives at the point where such knowledge is necessary in order to go further.

5. COMMUNICATION

The communication between school and parent, and between teachers and parents, must be total. Minimally, parents must routinely be apprised of attendance, tardies, discipline problems, career workshops, and homework assignments. Knowledge about the first two constitutes an early warning system. According to the Department of Justice, 81 percent of current prison inmates were truants first. That jumps to 95 percent for juvenile offenders.

6. BENCHMARKING

Pre- and post-evaluation have to be set up in advance to determine to what extent if any the new system raises levels of student achievement. In addition, parent and student surveys need to be designed to determine to what extent changes in the family in general and in parent and student relationships in particular also have come about.

The value of putting the cart before the horse is that it makes explicit the challenge of what is needed and what has to be included if all the desirable goals are to be met. The obstacles of role coercion and of parental variability mentioned earlier hopefully have been addressed above. The sticking point of course is time. Many teachers do not even have the time to consult with their colleagues, let alone to develop parent participation plans. Thus freeing up teachers to sustain instructionally focused teacher–parent partnerships seems to be the key stumbling block and may doom entirely the prospect of its ever happening. But recent labor negotiations in England which bear on the question of available teacher time may suggest that there is light at the end of the tunnel.

Teachers in England work an average of fifty-two hours a week. (I suspect that does not include time at home correcting papers or preparing lesson plans.) Further analysis revealed that 16 percent of those hours were taken up with administrative and related matters. The goals? Reduce the total number of hours and increase teacher time with students in the classroom. The solution? Hire assistants to absorb some of the administrative work and to help teachers maximize their time with students. The cost of hiring the assistants is estimated to be $1.64 billion by 2005.

It is a dreadful solution. Any solution that costs that much, and introduces less qualified personnel into an instructional situation at a time when the search is in the other direction for highly qualified professionals, is really a bigger problem in disguise. It is thus not unlike the recent requests to hire administrative assistants so that principals could be freer to be instructional leaders. Money cannot be a variable leveraging agent. When it is used that way the solution has to be sent back to the drawing board.

If the challenge was put anew to administrators now and given the above design of what is needed, what can administrators do? Where and how can time be found? Three general directions present themselves. They range from review to self-restraint to radical surgery.

Taking a leaf from the English analysis, examine to what extent teachers are involved in administrative and related matters. Equally as important, determine specifically what it consists of and how much of that can be removed, outsourced, done electronically, and above all questioned as to whether it should be assigned in the first place. Although done initially on a school basis, the findings and above all the solutions might be districtwide.

The second step involves self-review. If time saved and gained became a ruling priority of principals, then it behooves them to pause every time they are contemplating a new initiative that is not mandated, to question whether it should be done at all or in a way that consumes teacher time and energy. One example may suffice. The school board in one of its freewheeling sessions discussed whether kids were happy in school. An enterprising principal asks all his teachers to meet with each of their students in homeroom and social studies classrooms to discuss whether they were happy or not and why. Imagine some of the reactions and colorful language of teachers that greeted that request! Principals should anticipate teacher reactions and increasingly become stewards not only of the budget, but also of time as an invaluable resource. Some may note at this point that the time savings are piddling so far; they are more morale boosters than real time-savers. Not so the next initiative, which radically goes for the jugular.

Before going ahead let us once again set the scene and identify both the variables and the constants. The goal is to find the time for teachers to work with two sets of partners: their grade-level and subject matter colleagues and parents. The first is sometimes done, but not as often, and certainly not as thoroughly as to ensure a collaborative difference. Such interactions in effect constitute professional development. The second is totally new, time-consuming, and labor-intensive.

What is fixed in place is the teacher's schedule: the number of classes she is assigned and how often they meet. But suppose that became a variable instead of a constant? How persuaded are we that classes have to meet five days a week or all day? What would be the downside of such a reconfiguration? What would be done with the students not in class, especially at a time when high-stakes testing is demanding higher levels of performance? The answer: the same thing that their teachers and parents are doing: consulting and collaborating.

Students would be organized into smaller subject matter study groups, thus in effect reducing class size. Each study group would follow daily prescribed lesson plans and agendas. Time would be carefully monitored so that it fulfilled state standards of the minimum number of hours of instruction required. It would involve peer tutoring, and it would also be led at times by upper-class students and by parents and volunteers. Occasionally it would be computer-assisted, especially for test-prep skills.

Homework would be gone over collectively. Lists of student questions would be compiled and brought back as feedback to class for clarification.

A new category would be added to student evaluation: ability to work together and solve problems in teams. Such collaborative learning also could prepare for similar arrangements at home with siblings and parents. The model of student learning is familial. It emulates home-schooling. It stresses the group and what the group can do for each member that he or she may not be able to do for him- or herself. It easily accommodates character education as well as other curricula that require teams, such as service learning or project learning.

The gains would be multiple and considerable. It offers not one but a number of win-win gains. Enough to try it? to risk it? One way of making anything less radical is to make it experimental. Select a small group of teachers at one grade level or all involved in the same subject matter, and give them the objectives of saving time and what it would be used for. Costs cannot be increased, and additional people cannot be hired. Ask them to explore reducing class meeting times but continuing class objectives in smaller student groups that meet for the equivalent of time otherwise spent in class. Ask them finally to produce a design that would permit all this to happen and to calculate the net time gained. Finally, to provide further impetus to the effort, also announce the project to reduce administrative loads and to exercise self-restraint.

What is the worst that can happen? Time remains immovable. Nothing can be shifted around or reconfigured without serious slippage. We are stuck with what we have got. However, even if those were the conclusions, look at what has been gained: communicating the priority of teacher consultation with colleagues and parents, suggesting alternative ways students can learn, and recognizing the commitment of administrators to do something significant about their workloads. These are no small offsetting gains. But imagine a best-case scenario. Suppose it worked. Imagine if the above gains also became the drivers of school reconfiguration and produced a design in which time was an obedient servant rather than a tyrannical taskmaster; would that signal a new day for education? And would that not be worth the time to try? To parents it certainly would.

⑰

ADMINISTRATOR–PARENT
PARTNERSHIPS

Conversations with administrators during these tough times often generate a yearning for real leadership opportunities. After some justifiable venting, what usually follows is not so much how to deal with pressing and immediate problems but the question of what is coming down the pike. When I ask, why so futuristic? I usually get one of three answers:

1. "I want something big and distractive that will stand alone and draw attention away from all the crazy busy overwhelming details crowding in and demanding attention."
2. "I want to have the illusion of engaging something substantial and comprehensive that has not already been chewed on, spit out or predigested."
3. "I want leadership options that engage and break new ground so that I can lead for a change rather than being a manager of small potatoes."

Clearly, all the above responses may be variations on the same driving desire by administrators to be leaders, not just followers; to shape reform, not just obediently implement it; to create, not just apply change. They are right to yearn for such distinctions because in fact a review of the checklist of various leadership options yields few or slim pickings.

For example, accountability and standards leadership is already in the hands of NCLB; administrators are essentially enforcers or sadly, of late, apologizers. Instructional leadership on behalf of student achievement is chancy; one can bet on the wrong curriculum model or advocate stringent rubrics that carry with them a 50 percent failure rate. Advocacy of anything alternative, whether teacher or supervisor certification, or hiring incentives or performance bonuses, runs the risk of championing solutions that may turn out to produce bigger problems. Even the recent and heady call by William Ouchi (2003) for principals to become entrepreneurs may create more leadership options for teachers than for administrators. However, there is one area that is generally overlooked and that is ripe for leadership: parents.

Why parents? There are at least three reasons:

1. Political:
They are a major constituency and perhaps the most important and desirable taxpaying allies administrators can find.
2. Major Players:
They are sanctioned as central by NCLB. In addition, many PTAs have created fund-raising foundations to support education. In one school district in Oregon, when budget restrictions resulted in termination of a popular teacher, the PTA raised enough money to hire her back.
3. Learning Partners:
It is becoming increasingly clear that the kinds of student gains required, within tight timelines, and the numbers involved cannot be accomplished by teachers and school alone; and that without the involvement and structured partnership of parents and the home all will fall short, or gains once made will not last.

If the above is sufficiently persuasive, then like all leadership challenges the options range from the minimum to the maximum to the optimum. The flexible part is that each subsequent stage subsumes the former one; the hard part is that the progression from one to the other becomes more difficult and ups the leadership ante.

THE MINIMUM: THE LEADERSHIP OF COMMUNICATIONS

Advocacy takes the form of building a new series of information bridges between school and home, educators and parents. This is particularly needed in the area of NCLB, because according to the recent Gallup poll, only 6 percent indicated that they know a great deal about its provisions, but over 76 percent knew nothing or very little. If at all possible, administrators want to avoid or reduce the kinds of outcries and court cases that occurred when 6,000 students in Massachusetts failed the graduation exam and were denied their diplomas, and when 4,000 third graders in Dade County, Florida, were told they would have to be left back. Sidestepping such public relations nightmares and working with the local PTA, principals need to set up workshops on NCLB 101 and appear before parents on a regular basis to secure their support and involvement. Above all, leadership should be exercised on putting in place an electronic information system between the school and home, and on providing workshops for teachers to utilize effectively the new set of virtual relationships. Florida just installed the Virtual Counselor, which provides parental access to all student records going back to kindergarten. The communication goal, in short, is leadership on behalf of total transparency. Recently, an enterprising principal in Denver introduced numerous home visits to enhance the communication relationships between home and school.

THE MAXIMUM: THE LEADERSHIP OF LEARNING PARTNERSHIPS

For parents to be really involved, their roles and assignments have to be specifically planned, assigned, and followed up. Moreover, that can only be done by the teachers of their kids. In other words, for the school and the home to work in tandem, each lesson plan must be accompanied or multiplied by as many sub-lesson plans as there are students in the class. Differentiation of instruction in class must now also find expression in differentiation of home and homework assignments. If parents are in effect to be extensions of the school, they must be given the same kind of specific and individualized guidance and direction one would give any fellow teacher, or in this instance co-teacher.

Clearly, that is a lovely ideal, but when would teachers do that? Where would the time be found for such labors? In fact, one can step back and claim that time in general does not support three critical tasks and interactions likely to impact student achievement: sharing of lesson plans by grade level and/or subject by teachers; collaborative review and diagnosis of student work; and now, development of follow-up lessons for and occasionally with parents. If ever a situation cried out for leadership intervention, this one does. Moreover, because all three activities are so unarguably and interactively needed, the failure to facilitate their happening suggests a failure of leadership nerve or commitment. If it is true that where there is will there is a way, what is the way leadership has to find?

The key to innovative problem solving is to treat what is fixed as a variable. For example, why must every subject be scheduled daily? Suppose instead it is offered three rather than five times a week. Would that provide the time necessary for the three tasks? Surely, but immediately, the fear of unsupervised students two days a week loosed on the school strikes terror into everyone's heart. But who said they were to be abandoned or left without structure? Teachers would group them into study and work teams; lessons would be prepared or computer assignments provided in advance. Coaches accustomed to run study tables for athletes would provide group dynamics and conflict negotiation skills 101. Unannounced, every once in a while their teachers would visit and provide further instruction on the benefits of cooperative learning. It not only would work, but also provide more novelty and group growth than the traditional arrangement. Innovative leadership would have created a win-win situation.

THE OPTIMUM: EDUCATION PLANNING CLEARINGHOUSE

It is unfortunate but true that competition has not been happily embraced by many educators. Some principals have publicly or privately attacked charter schools, challenged the loss of socialization of homeschools and cyberschools, and questioned the claims of gains and cost savings of private management companies. Naturally, each one attacked or minimized has replied with equal vigor and venom. The result is a very ugly public scene of educators fighting educators and the martyrdom of each side claiming its ox is gored more than the other. Meanwhile, no attention or guidance is being provided to parents and their offspring, faced with an incredible range of different school choices, along an extensive range from K–16, and beset along the way with NCLB-mandated tests, including one for technological competence by 2006.

The clear-cut leadership option is to elect the high road of professional service rather than the low road of squabbling competition. Instead of fighting over education providers, the focus needs to be shifted to the needs of students and questions of parents. Moreover, it has to be a dynamic because kids and families change, and what is the best choice for the middle school experience might not be the best one for high school. In short, leadership requires that schools—ideally school districts—offer parents and their kids a comprehensive planning support service that would not be unlike and in fact include college search planning.

The two immediate problems that would have to be solved are competence and costs: having available and putting in place trained counselors and paying the additional costs of providing the service. Both issues are solvable in many different ways and need to be left in the hands of local leaders to develop in their communities. Hopefully all solutions would have at least one factor in common; because this is an educational activity, it should always center on learning. In other words, the planning exercise should always be a self-defining and developmental planning experience for both kids and families. That way they too can play follow the leader, especially with those administrators who in fact helped to make planning their future together possible in the first place.

Leadership unneeded? Undervalued? Unwelcome? Not by a long shot. Try giving parents and their kids new options—changing student-centered to student- and parent-driven, bringing the community from outside to inside the gates, and making school and home not alternatives, but versions of each other. Such a legacy of leadership would ensure that no child is left unknown, unengaged, and undeveloped.

Part 5

THE HOME AS OPERATIONS CENTER

In the previous section the emphasis was on the parent as a master planner. Now that role has to be expanded to include learning manager and broker. Some will immediately object to turning the home, which is supposed to be primarily a safe and loving place, into a business operational center. However, using homeschooling as a model, the home has to be both a caring and learning place. Moreover, it has to be efficient and agile because it now has to deal with, engage with, and be responsive to not only different kinds of parents, their needs, and their life and work styles, but also all the differences of their kids and of their schooling. Finally, the basic family is often no longer the same.

The current range of parents includes:

- Two-income families: they have no choice but to run their home as a tight ship.
- Single-parent moms or dads: even more so.
- Stay-at-home moms (and dads): more leisure but usually more activities and carpooling.
- Grandparents raising grandkids: generationally sometimes at odds and needing firm direction.

Necessity and preference also influence the focus on home management. Parents, needing to go to work or desiring to have a career, come
together in their common need for kids not to have to suffer because of
adult choices. In addition to help with planning, parents also need to be
aware of what typically is now needed for the home to be an operations
center and guidance system.

⑱

THE HOME AS OPERATIONS CENTER

Much can be learned about social and family changes from changes in home design. The living room generally has been replaced by the family room (sometimes called the great room). In some homes that subsequently has been converted by technology into an entertainment center. The spare bedroom or finished basement has become totally or in part an office or workspace and/or workout area for parents, later sometimes for kids as well. It often contains minimally a phone, computer, printer, fax machine, scanner, and digital camera.

In some cases, parents work at home, full- or part-time, or telecommunicate to their jobs part of the time. Many parents have careers that require them to remain constantly in touch with their office or clients; they never go anywhere without cell phones or pagers. Clearly, technology has played a major role in home design and in living and work patterns. It also clearly has affected kids and the way they learn.

THE DIGITAL GENERATION

The current generation is the first to be raised under the total aegis of the computer. It is also the most electronically wired group to date.

Many have their own computers, laptops, Palm Pilots, cell phones, digital cameras, home entertainment systems, portable and fixed Game Boys, and so on. Of course, many homes do not have all the toys, but most kids have computer access, minimally at school.

Technology already has been integrated into the curriculum. Many textbooks come with CDs. Colleges routinely have signaled the transformation of traditional courses by using new prefixes: economics is now e-economics, English e-English. In fact, most college Comp 101 courses now require that at least 50 percent of research sources be Internet-based, which is followed then by a new way of documenting electronic citations.

Such practices are increasingly being implemented in high schools as well. A study of minority kids using the Internet showed a 30 percent increase in their reading skills. Then as noted earlier, parents have become part of electronic communication network services between school and home, teacher and individual parent. If the trend of parent–teacher partnerships further develops to the point where teacher lesson plans factor in home follow-up assignments and projects, and if accomplishing as well as monitoring such seamless relationships requires such exchanges, perhaps that should become part of a school–home link. In short, no home can be an effective learning center without providing even the most basic minimum technology.

A STUDY PLACE

Parents need to provide their children with a fixed and assured learning workplace. It may be their own rooms, or a common area like the finished basement, or even an infrequently used dining room. In many homes it is still the kitchen table before or after dinner. Wherever it is, it has to be dedicated space, and it should be respected as such by everyone and not be invaded or appropriated by anyone or anything else. That way learning and homework acquire high value and symbolic importance. Allocating space and time are family priorities.

Each study place also should be a monitoring and traffic station. There should be a large calendar on which all critical dates, activities, events, tests, and so on are recorded for both parents and kids. Updates should be daily, sometimes right after dinner and before homework or study time. Conflicts are to be immediately addressed and resolved. Minimally, the calendar should be six months out, in some cases a year ahead. Parents should routinely supplement the review of the events of the week by addressing lead times: when longer projects have to be started, what points they should reach by what date, when they should be finished to be looked over by parents before handing in. Students are to record such progressive steps as entries in their own individual school planners.

A place, ideally a table or cabinet, needs to be designated, and located just before the door leading in and out, as a drop-off and pick-up point. That is where empty lunch bags are dropped off and where full ones are picked up. A special bin is set aside for depositing all school communications, including notes or permission slips that have to be signed. It is there also where everything that has to go to school is to be picked up. The more things are well organized, the fewer occasions there are for last-minute hysterics, accusations of blame, and wild and wrenching searches before leaving the house on time with what each one needs. Kids should not leave for school unsettled or scattered. Some homes use old-fashioned entryway furniture with a bench seat/cabinet and hooks for clothes as their departure and arrival center. But whatever the choice it is the lynchpin of the entire operational center.

TEST PREP

With NCLB in place, kids are going to be tested again and again. Fearful of low scores being reported, teachers will not only pretest frequently, but also teach to the test. And if the scores are still too low, the curriculum may be stripped to only what is being tested. Art programs everywhere have been deleted entirely or reduced to token levels. How can parents and the home help their kids survive and do well in this nonstop testing onslaught?

Home test prep has to include three major dimensions: Test Design, Test Anticipation, and Drill Practice.

1. Test Design

Tests vary with subject matter. Questions take different forms. There are factual questions that are couched as blanks to be filled in, true or false, or multiple choice. The first is the hardest: you either know it or you don't. Such questions require a great deal of drill. With true or false there is the benefit of a fifty-fifty guessing average. Multiple choice offers the best opportunity to recognize the correct answer, although that advantage is cleverly offset by including tantalizingly near-correct other choices. However, using an elimination process can increase the odds.

Process subjects such as math require working out the answers according to acceptable formats. In fact, in many cases a significant amount of credit is given for the right format even though the answer may be incorrect. Finally, there are the essay questions usually required in language arts and social sciences. Students make the mistake of regarding these as opportunities to throw the bull. That will backfire. Students need to take a few minutes to develop a general outline of the main parts of the answer, and key facts, dates, and names should be placed alongside every main part.

Parents can help their kids by making them more self-conscious and aware of test design. Parents can compare testing to an interview situation and walk their kids through a test interview. Kids can be asked questions about the facts of their lives, to explain the process of schooling, to describe in detail a particularly meaningful learning experience. Best of all, kids can develop tests of their own, learning specifically what makes a good factual question, a challenging process question, and an essay question. They even may anticipate many of the questions on the test. In fact, because they have made up the test, the entire process may make more sense, even appear rational. The key is to make kids more self-conscious, critical, and reflective about the entire testing process. Forethought is forearmed. They have to become knowledgeable about their knowledge.

2. Test Anticipation

Studying and preparing for a test can best be done by making one up, which is another reason why knowledge of test design is important. The made-up test has to be cast in the actual form that they will encounter. When I was in college my best friend and I never studied together—we would laugh all the time and never get anything done—but each of us made up our version of the test and then shared it. We got so good at it that we routinely guessed 90–95 percent of the questions. We even considered selling our sample tests. How did we get such a batting average?

We did two things. First, we not only took good and complete class notes, but also followed a system of putting stars or asterisks all over the place when we thought it would be a test subject or question. In other words, if they have not taken good notes and used a code to earmark the key points, students are going into a fight with one hand already tied behind their backs. They can't use what they don't have. Second, we psyched out the teacher, which is really the human version of psyching out the test design. It suited our melodramatic purposes to make him or her a mean SOB out to get us. Our task was to outfox, outsmart, and outmanipulate such villainy. We tried to think like the teacher, bringing out the worst in him in the form of what questions he would diabolically pick to bedevil us; and if he had to choose between being fair or vicious, he would always go for the jugular. Thinking mean turned out to be thinking smart.

Test anticipation is the key. Parents can suggest not only that their kids do it, but also offer to take one that their kids made up. It is amazing how much kids enjoy the ignorance of their parents, but they also learn more by doing it, and believe their parents now also have a better idea of what they are up against.

3. Drill Practice

Obviously, there is no substitute for making sure you can recall what you know. There are many good computer drill programs. Parents can always be available when kids say, "Test me." Sometimes kids become creative. They list the words they always misspell on a roll of reinforced toilet paper to signify what it represents to them. They come up with acronyms to remember a series of names or places. They march around the room chanting dates. They use as many of the multiple intelligences as they can. However, memorization can be made more systematic and even scientific.

MEMORIZATION AND MEMORY AIDS AND PROMPTS

Cognitive psychologists and researchers have examined the brain's storage and retrieval system. In the process, distinctions have been made between short- and long-term memory. They also have found that there are three dimensions of memory in the brain:

- How memories are formed.
- How memories are stored.
- How memories are retrieved.

Many parents today—indeed, many cultures—were required to memorize extensively and to learn by rote. Long poems, the names of fifty states, the planets of the solar system, and so on, were committed to memory by entire classes chanting together. Although only a few still can recall and recite snatches of the original, generally it has been deleted from long-term memory. In other words, a rationale drives the initial formation of memory. If what was originally formed was coerced, mechanical, and often questionably relevant, its storage capacity is tenuous. Then too, when the original motivation or condition goes away or is superseded by another and more pressing situation, its retrieval power is severely diminished.

The problem that researchers generally have found with rote memorization is that it is not only unretentive, but also distractive. It deflects time and energy away from the principal task, which is to understand the information rather than to memorize it. The other problem is that it is often unnecessary. Why memorize what can be quickly looked up, especially elaborate math formulas when they are already stored inside sophisticated calculators? Indeed, why memorize altogether?

Certain tests and tasks require it. Organization of life and work make it a daily and even hourly routine. Wall calendars, executive and student planners, and now palm recorders are devices that regulate and monitor future events that keep us on track and on time. In short, memory, as well as the various ways we manage and turn it over to other mechanisms of recall, determines effectiveness. It also determines student success.

I remember the parting conversation I had with my dissertation advisor just before graduation. At Johns Hopkins we were trained to be publishing researchers. He said, "The first five years you can draw upon your brain and memory materials for writing articles. After that, you need a good filing system. That will determine your future success. Lacking that you will fizzle out."

Of course he was both right and wrong. He was right about long-term success, which requires systems or mechanisms to store, house, and above all integrate what is known. It is the brain in a file case. However, he was wrong in two other ways. First, every system can be personalized and individualized. Thus, I found ways to keep alive the often chaotic fertility of the first five years. That was where the joy of research comes from, which I was determined not to lose. Second, when memory is stirred and prodded, not in any demanding, but in speculative ways, it can cross over to and even merge with intellectual and creative channels. It can form alliances that extend and stretch recollection beyond its boundaries and lead it to new perspectives and discoveries. Above all, what the advice of my mentor dramatized is that memory and its many productive and necessary connections are too important for professional achievement in general, and student success in particular, not to be examined and systematically stored and used, especially because effective memorization is seldom taught in schools.

MEMORY ENHANCEMENT TECHNIQUES

Five techniques can be used:

1. Use all sensory modalities: sight, sound, touch, smell, etc.—in short, Multiple Intelligences.
2. We remember best what we want to—what is interesting and useful, what is curious and practical.
3. Link the new to what is already known and stored. Give it something already strong and in place to hold on to. Relate the new to one already there.
4. Individualize and personalize memory systems and aids, especially if they are creative and strike your fancy.
5. Use story, narrative, incident, and conversations as storage containers. They are inherently memorable. They also have crossover power to stir connections and innovation.

Do they work and produce results? In 1990–1991, a special memory enhancement program, the Christa McAuliffe Fellowship, raised reading performance by 15 percentile points and math by 14. What was used and found to be effective?

THE THREE S'S OF EFFECTIVE MEMORIZATION

Sound, sight, and story. These are what support and sustain not only memory but student success. In other words, minimally there are now three chances to remember something. Here is how each one works and how parents can help their kids better prepare for tests and homework. Although students may develop preferences, it is important to keep the whole battery of aids active and available. Kids change as they develop, and last year's rejected verbal dramatics may be this year's savior. Moreover, these three amplifications address all three memory modes: formation, storage, and retrieval. Here then is how each of these three S's works and can be used by parents at home to help their kids with knowledge acquisition and retention, and with test prep.

Sound

Reading and studying usually are silent and isolated. That can be stultifying and stupefying; one can be lulled into passivity and the words become blurred. One antidote is reading out loud, especially selective passages. To focus students on the task, parents should ask them to identify at least one big and one small new idea that they learned in their reading, and to test and single out those big and small new ideas by reading them aloud, first to themselves, and then to their parents. That forms memory, gives it retentive power, and finally provides a sound cue for its retrieval. It also shifts monologue to dialogue, especially when parents become players and join in the discussion.

Sound also can be used to help memorize dates or names for a test. Kids often march around musically drilling the data into their heads with rhythm and chant. Some teachers tap the musical process of call and response used in many religious services when the congregation musically and immediately responds to the challenge of the leader.

Mnemonics are a favorite device with all sorts of personal variations. It is a process of using the first letter of a made-up verse or sentence to help you remember a list of things. For example, to make sure the word "diarrhea" is correctly spelled the following mnemonic is appropriately created: "Dashing In A Rush Running Harder Else Accident." Students should be encouraged to use that memory aid, especially for lists. Some have even become favorites, such as Roy G Biv for the colors of the rainbow: Red, Orange, Yellow, and Green. Blue, Indigo, and Violet.

Parents and kids who are musical can transform the memorization of dull and boring facts into a performance. Drama not only makes the task fun and less onerous, but scripts can also animate and bring to life abstract ideas. Parents and their kids can afford to be outrageous at home, especially when things may be dull and grim at school.

Sight

Reading also can be enlivened and yield its secrets by highlighting—by using a colored pen to underscore important or big ideas, especially those that may be on a test. Parents should encourage their kids to be aggressive visual readers. Three different colors can be used according to a code: yellow for important ideas to understand and remember; red for facts and dates; and blue for possible test questions. Where the textbooks are supplied by the school and have to be returned, parents may consider investing in extra copies to be marked up. Often they are available, used but unmarked, from Amazon.com at reduced prices.

Parents also should encourage their kids to develop even more complex and elaborate visual learning codes and annotations. It can become their own created language. In fact, in some homes it is a family exercise. Everyone sits down and puts together a common legend. Thus, in the margin of a text or a written composition some of the following equivalents might appear:

?	=	Not clear
!	=	Big idea
✻	=	Possible test question
%	=	Playing the Percentages
L	=	Link to_____
BS	=	Baloney Stuff
$	=	Reward for an A

In surveys the clear preference is for various visual devices and visual thinking. That ranges from writing things down in a student planner to making notes on the palm of the non-writing arm. Students retain and understand more when they take notes on what they have read. Highlighting and marginal notes speed up the process. But an equally valued and more creative approach is to ask your kids to process thoughts and ideas through their spatial intelligence.

Specifically, ask your kids to draw a picture of an abstract idea. Give the example of Justice, which is pictured as wearing blindfolds and holding a balance scale. Ask them how that powerfully defines justice. Then ask them to render another abstract idea, such as the U.S., visually.

Introduce them also to graphs, pie charts, diagrams, tables, and so on, as visual ways of not only presenting, but also understanding information. Teach them the summary power of a matrix. Ask them to construct one. If one already exists, ask them to examine how a rubric of writing performance is put together and how it measures progress and rates needing improvement. Here is a sample rubric for composition:

Component	Performance Levels	Mastery	Adequate	Needing Improvement
Organization				
Transitions				
Spelling				

After constructing such a rubric or examining one supplied in class, take the next step and ask your kids to apply it to their own writing. In effect, ask them to assess their own work and give themselves a grade. If they invite you to do the same, you then can compare notes. The advantage of such comparative visual self-assessment is that it usually dramatizes what needs to be revised and improved, and what can be left alone. This self-correcting and self-learning exercise is seldom used in school, mostly because teachers value control and dominance. Thus, in this case parents can give their kids a competitive advantage.

There are so many ways to once again confirm the old wisdom that a picture is worth a thousand words. Repetition and endless drill with words frequently misspelled is not nearly as effective as isolating visually the offending letter or letters. Thus, the standard mistake is using "e" instead of "a." The corrective is to write the word this way—"sepArate"— to exaggerate and thus impress it in memory; the scale of the right letter acts as the corrective. It works every time.

Story

Motivational speakers always tell stories. They dramatize the lows and highs, failures and successes of their lives The first registers vulnerabiliy; the second salutes triumphing over adversity. The former invites common identification with everyone in the audience; the latter sets the motivated apart and draws them closer to the inner circle of the speaker. It is regularly effective.

Why? Because story has great power. Before we knew how to read, it was a magical time and place when our parents or older siblings read to us. But such power is not limited to childhood. Even the famous Harvard MBA program is based on case studies, which are really stories about particular businesses. Strategic plans are often rendered as scenarios, which are scripts of future events. The value of working in teams is often taught through disaster simulations, which dramatize how a group has to work together to survive. In short, case studies, scenarios, and simulations are effective because meaning is conveyed through charged situations and a cast of characters acting out and speaking their separate and shared differences.

How can the power of story be tapped and made a part of the home learning process? All history and the social sciences are basically stories that were then converted into often pompous concepts, dull facts, and endless dates. Students can reverse the process and recreate the stories of the people who made events happen. Effective teachers have dressed up as historical figures and, assuming their identities, acted out historical events. Another technique is to simulate a news program in ancient Greece, for example, that broadcasts the fall of Troy or the suicide of Socrates.

How can story engage math and chemistry? It can do this through the drama of relationships. A theorem or a formula is essentially held together by the glue of commonality. The different parts are like characters who are drawn or repelled by each other. Students can animate the different parts of a formula by having them speak about their separate chemical characteristics (sodium and chloride), and then describing the process of bringing them together to form a new compound (salt).

Once parents introduce this different way of studying, understanding, and memorizing math and science—in fact, all subjects—and their kids catch on, it will take off on its own. Knowledge will be dramatized, and it will be retained because it will be memorable, and because it bears the personal stamp of their own creativity. Story will function as a creative mnemonic, triggering recall.

RETRIEVAL CUES AND THE FORGETTING CURVE

Current brain research has developed an elaborate and complex profile of what cues work best with both short- and long-term memory, and why some memories are blurred, fragmented, and finally lost. However, in terms of parental guidance and student success, it all boils down to the following five guidelines:

1. Initial learning and memorization must be strong for encoding to take place. Otherwise forgetting occurs almost immediately.
2. Memory must be regularly stirred to be kept alive.
3. Drill and practice serve constantly to reinstate original memory and learning.
4. Memory linked to other or new memories gains a new lease on life and its vital connections.
5. The most powerful source of memory formation, storage, and retrieval is relevance and meaningfulness. Using, sight, sound, and story makes the learning not only generically more accessible, but also personally more identifiable.

If parents, using the knowledge of brain research and the techniques of memorization, can help their kids not only to learn but also liberate them into becoming active learners and putting their own stamp on their learning, they will have presided over the birth of lifelong learners. In short, what is at stake in the home is your kids' future.

The only other issue that matches test prep, studying, and memorization at home in intensity and importance is homework, which is why it is being treated separately in a chapter all its own.

19

HOMEWORK AND HOMESCHOOLING

The subject of homework is all over the map. Some teachers—indeed some schools—are almost compulsive about it. They give assignments every day, which often require one to two hours each night to complete. Then the contradictions begin. Many teachers do not always check or collect the homework, and those that do often return it unmarked except for a quick check at the top of the page.

Teachers who lament that their students do not do their homework or take it seriously give the homework during class time. That strange practice, aside from giving the teacher an unscheduled break, helps to explain why, when students are quizzed by parents about having any homework, they answer correctly that they did it in school. In short, some give no or little homework, while others pour it on. In fact, a perverse measure often is developed by some parents: the best teachers give the most homework.

The lack of conformity or even intelligence of homework assignments usually signifies three patterns: lack of homework training of teachers; lazy teachers taking the easy way out or overbearing ones being punitive; and the absence of a distictwide homework policy. With the last, parents at least have leverage.

SCHOOL HOMEWORK POLICY

If a school does not have such a policy, here is a model of one that parents might wish to support. Generally, homework policies have four main sections: a general statement of purpose; general goals of guidelines; specific guidelines for teachers; and specific guidelines for parents.

General Statement of Purpose

1. The purpose of homework is to raise levels of student achievement.
2. Homework teaches students to be independent learners.
3. Homework should be designed to relate directly to and extend class work.
4. Teachers should carefully prepare homework assignments, thoroughly explain what is required, and provide prompt comments when the work is completed.

General Goals of the Guidelines

1. To promote conformity and consistency of assignments throughout the district.
2. To help new teachers understand and adjust to district guidelines.
3. To facilitate and enhance communication between school and home, teachers and parents.
4. To provide parents with an opportunity to become directly involved in their child's learning.
5. To encourage parents to help develop students' good study habits and effective time on task.

Teacher Guidelines

1. Homework should always be related to specific class subjects.
2. Homework should not be used to introduce new material.
3. Overload should be avoided.

4. Homework should be differentiated to minister to different student abilities.
5. Teachers also should be cognizant of after-school time variables of athletics, extracurricular activities, music lessons, and so on, as well as the extent of home and family support.
6. All tasks should be explained clearly. Ideally, written instructions should accompany homework. That would also ensure that the parents have a clear understanding of what is being assigned.
7. Homework should be collected by the teacher, graded, and returned in a timely fashion.
8. Students should record assignments in their student planner, which should be reviewed periodically by the teacher and daily by parents.
9. When homework assignments are consistently not being completed, a conference should be scheduled between teacher and parents, and an appropriate plan of action should be developed.
10. The following time frames are given as guidelines:

(What follows are the recommendations of the National Parent Teachers Association.)

Grade Levels	Recommendations
K–2	10–20 minutes of homework
3–6	30–60 minutes
6–8	60–90 minutes
8–12	1–2 hours
12–16	2–3 hours

Parent Guidelines and Goals

1. Maintain high expectations of performance at home.
2. Monitor time on task and completion rates.
3. Maintain a homework journal to record observations of problem-solving modes, organizational skills, extent and nature of test prep, and so on.
4. Discuss journal entries during teacher–parent conferences.
5. Provide designated, consistent, and nondistractive places to study.

6. Review assignments before and after.
7. Make sure students do what is asked and in acceptable form.
8. Set aside set times for doing homework.
9. Stock necessary supplies.
10. Check computer time and use to insure relevance to tasks.

THE PARENTAL HOMEWORK JOURNAL

It is recommended that parents keep a homework journal. Although time-consuming, it will yield important dividends. However, it requires discipline: parents need to be objective and nonjudgmental. They have to record data like scientists. Its goal is to assemble a profile of student performance doing schoolwork at home. It records behaviors, study habits, time management and organizational skills, completion rates, quality of work, and so on. It is to be used as a home benchmark of where the student is at, and as such it can be shared at teacher–parent conferences, so that both can compare notes on student performance in school and at home. By bringing both halves together, a more complete portrait can better support diagnostically driven correctives and interventions. Here is a sample of a series of observations and entries in the Parent Homework Journal (PHJ):

- Time: When started and when finished.
- Place: Where worked, location changes if any, and why?
- Date: Of this entry.
- List of assignments and due dates.
- Student estimates of how long each will take.
- Record of how long it actually takes.
- Getting-started difficulties, completion difficulties.
- Subjects preferred, those avoided.
- Deflections and distractions.
- Nature of conversations with parents about difficulties or frustrations.
- Review of quality of completed work.
- Assignment of three grades: Great, OK, and Redo. The last is non-negotiable; the second is optional.

Recording the above observations initially may be tedious, but with time and practice they can yield significant results. In addition to providing parents with an even playing field with teachers, parents can make their own decisions about the ways students work at home and whether tutoring and time management skills would be helpful.

Zeroing in on specific subject matter difficulties, parents can secure tutors or tap the extended support of Multiple Intelligences that, although not used in school, may offer equally effective alternative routes to mastery. Above all, the journal puts parents in the driver's seat. It provides the observational data not only for school communication, but also for home action.

If signs of school difficulty or disengagement begin to appear, parents should not adopt the typical school's attitude of "Let's wait and see." They should move immediately to arrest and to turn that negativity around. Schools and teachers are always reluctant to admit failure, let alone that they may have contributed to or caused it. But parents are not involved—nor should they be—in such image or public relations problems. They are rescuers, if that is what is required, or providers of enhancement and enrichment. Their task is to save and stimulate, or to save in order to stimulate. The journal not only diagnoses and supports such decisions, but also provides the means to measure the extent to which the remedies take hold and achieve both learning and family goals. It is thus an investment in the future success of kids in school and at home, and in the viability and quality of family life.

THE RESEARCH ON HOMEWORK

The research shows that in general shorter and more frequent assignments are more effective than longer assignments. This particularly applies to math homework. The number of examples should not be endless to make a point. Because state math testing now begins in the third grade, math homework correspondingly will increase in that grade.

The reasons for urging shorter assignments are not hard to find. Completion is a motivator. Being able to finish in relatively little time gives kids a sense of satisfaction and success and builds self-worth. Also, students are conditioned by time in class. If classes typically last forty to forty-five minutes and if homework assignments per subject matter go way beyond that, students may become rebellious, and regard them as excessive and even pointless. Teachers should never risk that kind of alienation.

The time spans noted above by grade levels generally do not include reading assignments, which can exceed the recommended limits. Reading, especially for elementary school kids, is regarded as the most important home activity, whether assigned or not. In this instance, parents, not the teacher, play the more important role; the home becomes the school.

For example, a significant research project is the one conducted by Johns Hopkins and entitled TIPS (Teachers Involve Parents in Schoolwork). What sets TIPS apart is that it is both a research and applied project. It studies and documents focused interventions. What is different and special about TIPS?

- Homework is designed from the outset by teachers to directly involve parent participation.
- The parental role is thus built in. It is not an option.
- Ideally, homework taps after-school advantages, accesses, and resources the classroom does not possess, and which require the help of parents.
- Actively and directly involved, parents specifically become aware of what is going on at school and what its demands and expectations are.
- Such knowledge serves as a home reality check.
- Teachers in turn develop a better and more specific understanding of what parents can contribute to a mutual learning process.
- Both teachers and parents can reinforce each other's efforts and work in tandem rather than at cross-purposes.

What did TIPS achieve? Here are the evaluations:

- Students: improved performance in general and writing skills in particular, reflected in higher grades and levels of satisfaction.

- TIPS was better than regular homework.
- Teachers: amplified their knowledge of the way their students work and think; witnessed greater mastery of subject matter; and increased communication of school goals and activities.
- Parents: found great value, importance, and affirmation in being made a dedicated and discrete part of the learning continuum, and in partnering with teachers. About 90 percent of parents wanted TIPS to continue.

DIFFERENT KINDS OF HOMEWORK

Because homework varies and comes at different times and lengths, it needs to have clear-cut foci. In general, homework is of five types:

1. Practice: to reinforce skills mastery.
2. Prep: to anticipate and prepare for tests.
3. Anticipation: to prepare for future lessons and introduction of new materials.
4. Extension: to apply skills and concepts to new areas not covered in class.
5. Integration: to demonstrate capacity to pull together materials and information into a unified whole, as may be required of a book report or science project.

HOMEWORK AND THE ROLE OF PARENTS

With respect to the above, parents should pick their battles and times of intervention. They also have to build a trusting relationship with their kids, so that they in turn feel comfortable asking for help. Also, parents have to run an open-door policy at home, so that when kids approach with books in hand and either a pleading or beaten look on their faces, parents are available and can seize and prize the moment for what it can offer both parent and kid.

Recognize that what is at stake is potential turnaround. Homework can create a little crisis which threatens their kids' image of whether they are smart and can succeed. If that sadly is not always a happy experience in school, it has to be so at home; otherwise there is no difference between the two.

The parent needs minimally to offer five things: reassurance, time availability, diagnostics, learning, and colearning or elbow teaching. The two extremes to avoid are overconfidence or overpraise—"Oh, I am sure you are smart enough to do this" or "A smart kid like you can't possibly be thrown by a little math problem"—or stepping in and completing the assignments and then saying triumphantly: "See how easy it is? Now you go ahead and do the rest on your own."

- Reassurance means that you are there to help: "Of course, I will try to help you."
- Time availability: "And we can take as much time as you need. I am free."
- Diagnostics: "Now let's see. What do you think the problem is here?"
- Learning: "I am not sure I know as much as you do about the way you do math now, and I don't want to mix you up with my old ways. Could you explain to me what is involved here?"
- Colearning: "I think I understand it better; you did an excellent job of teaching me. Now let us get back to the problem you are stuck on and see if we can work our way through it."

Many parents throw in the towel early on, especially with older kids, because they feel out of their depth. They do not feel confident in their own knowledge of the subject—perhaps they never did when they were in school. They also are rightly concerned that they may suggest ways of doing things which are at odds with current methodologies. But the parental technique recommended here and reflected in the above remarks of the parent is that of inquiry, not mastery. The temptation to be Super Mom or Dad, who knows it all, puts your needs as adults before those of your kids. Your image is not at stake, theirs is.

Strange as it may seem, homework epitomizes familial relationships. It is where the home not only becomes the school, but also the best kind of school, and where the parents become not only the teacher, but also the best kind of teacher. If regular school and teachers are great, then the home is a happy extension of both. If they are unevenly so, then the home has to be balanced and consistent. If they are dreadful, then the home has to be the antidote and corrective. If they are intellectually limited or impoverished, then the home has to offer the alternatives of Gardner's multiple intelligences. Above all, raising children is not child's play. It is adult's play. The stakes are often so high—witness the specter of failure raised by Glasser—that many parents take a step they never contemplated: homeschooling their kids—totally bringing together school and home, teacher and parent. Although not all homes and parents elect that option, as a model it should not only be admired, but also used, particularly in the ways parents manage homework.

DEVELOPING A HOMEWORK PLAN AND SYSTEM

Parents need to talk over how the home can be a school and how they can be teachers, colearners, and coaches. Then that has to be put in the form of a plan of principles and activities and a systemic way of making all that happen. Here is a suggested list:

Principles

- Homework is a family activity.
- Time is always available for help.
- Learning, reading, and studying are high priorities, much higher than watching TV or playing video games.
- One size fits all does not apply. Each kid is different.
- Home and school are not enemies but allies.

Operations

- Homework is not only about academics but also time management.
- Good time management of the home itself sets the standard for kids.
- Have kids relax and play when they come home from school.
- Customize study and homework plans to accommodate difference.

- Negotiate sibling conflicts: have the one who loves to play music wear earphones so that his sister who prefers silence can do her homework.
- The kitchen can often be a homework center before and immediately after dinner. Kids can talk to parents while dinner is being prepared. Then they all can spend an hour or so together afterward.
- Some homes arrange a "Family Work Hour" where kids and parents sit together. The kids do their homework; the parents do their bills or read.
- Keep the home well stocked with school supplies and poster boards, etc. Avoid last-minute runs to the store. Kids go ballistic when they can't find a pencil with an eraser to do their math homework.
- If a kid is struggling and losing ground with a particular subject like calculus or chemistry, and the help you have given or alternatives you have provided are not working, don't delay. Get a tutor. In some instances, make it easy on the budget by using a teenage babysitter who is good in these subjects.
- If it seems to be working and producing good results, don't discontinue it too quickly. Bad habits or misconceptions need time to be driven out by good habits as correctives.
- Informally and discreetly monitor and maintain a time log on each kid. Consider enrolling your kids in an after-school or online time management and study habits class. Any time such help can be provided by experts and by people other than parents, that gives parents a fresh start or blank page to work with. It also gives kids a welcome edge over their parents.
- Be prepared to be asked regularly by kids to justify studying this subject or that, and doing this kind of homework. Kids push for relevance, especially when they don't like what they are doing, have done poorly in certain subjects, and when the homework is heavy and sheer drudgery. Parents should be ready to respond in three ways. They can provide some examples of relevance. Lacking any, they can ask what the teacher said when asked that. Or finally they can fall back on the traditional foundations or building block examples, as in fact may have happened earlier when they first learned how to read or calculate. Above all, parents should not dismiss such requests, even if they believe they are deflective; they

should be respected and treated as signs of intellectual strengths. They certainly should not be given the curt dismissal of "Grit your teeth, get through it as best you can, and you will understand later why it had to be done this way." Chances are that later your kid may conclude that it was an even dumber way of doing things than he originally thought.

- Finally, parents need to recognize that homework provides a rare—in some cases the only—opportunity to see how their kids learn and think, organize their time, and master subjects and skills. Aside from helping them and designing a homework plan and system that reflects such observations, parents, perhaps without realizing it, are basically preparing themselves for more interactive conferences with teachers later on. Consider all that parents can now talk about; all the data and observations now recorded in their journal that they can now share; and above all, all the information that the teacher who is not at home and does not go over homework does not have. If there was ever an area that brings together home and school, teacher and parent, it is, surprisingly, homework. Parents need to work hard and smart to keep that bridge in place and to make sure that the traffic remains two-way.

REPORT CARDS

The next chapter deals with an old problem, but now with a new solution. The problem is report cards and how parents react to grades. Although that still remains a critical issue, it may become a different problem, given the prospect of new report cards being designed to reflect the new demands and data tracking of NCLB. For better or for worse, parents will now know more about their children's performance than ever before. To some parents the new report card may read like a medical report or a factory master process sheet with elaborate metrics and statistics. It may appear dense and opaque, written in a foreign language and intimidating. To others it may be a new and welcome full profile of their kid's performance patterns.

My argument is that parents have to know about, understand, and embrace this new technologically amplified report card, because it supports and extends what parents need to know if they are to develop and design their own home support and learning center and system. For the first time what the teacher and the school know is also what the parents do. More genuine teacher and parent partnerships thus can take place; and more opportunities for colearning between teachers and parents and between parents and their kids can be optimized. It's a win-win-win situation. However, before turning to report cards, it is important to bring to the surface the family's belief system, which undergirds testing, studying, and homework—all that is done and valued at home.

CODE OF THE HOME

Some homes not only develop, but also display what they stand for. They function like a vision and mission statement. Good ones are always aspirational; they are goals to shoot for and hopefully attain. Ideally, they should be drafted by both parents and kids and revisited, especially as kids grow older. It should not be a dated but a living code that changes as the family does. It should minimally be reviewed annually, especially just before school starts off again. If it genuinely reflects family values and relationships, it can be referred to or quoted regularly to resolve family disputes or differences of opinion. Here is one suggested version, which hopefully summarizes and incorporates many of the essentials discussed in this chapter:

- Education and Learning: It is what makes us human, what facilitates communication and personal growth. As Plato noted, "The life which is unexamined is not worth living."
- Choice: There are always options; there are always multiple ways of learning (MI); there are always, according to Glasser, choices parents need to offer children and themselves. The best choices are always those that ascend. The road taken should be the one urged by Robert Frost: the one less traveled by or its multiple versions, according to MI.
- Praise and Recognition: Replace put-downs with put-ups, acknowledge achievement but stress stretch, and above all individualize and custom-fit recognition. One size does not in fact fit all.

- Rituals: Create, maintain, preserve, and celebrate family rituals: bedtime reading, family dinners, pizza and movies nights at the start of and end of school terms, community volunteer projects, and so on. Be open to new ones, especially when suggested by kids.
- Imitation: Parents have to model the behaviors they seek in their kids and practice what they preach. In other words, they have to walk the talk. Kids need to see their parents read and discuss with each other what they are asking their kids to do. They also have to involve their kids in family activities such as going to the library or Barnes and Noble or Borders, balancing their checkbooks and the family budgets, going shopping, preparing meals, checking the calendar, accepting assignments to do Internet research on family vacations, using maps to figure out where they are going, how to get there, or generally where things are (building spatial intelligence), and so on.
- Patience and the Big Picture: For many, including some parents, the longest way around may turn out to be the shortest way home. Parents should not provide or approve shortcuts or quick fixes. They also cannot offer guarantees of success or forestall disappointment. All they can do is sketch out the big picture and project the impact of current decisions on the future. Other than that, parents have to trust their kids, be aware of the hurdles and opportunities of growing up, and be ready to assist them if they falter. They should never say "I told you so! I warned you!" That is the false superiority of know-it-all parents.
- Acceptance: Parents have to accept who and what their kids are and not hanker after or constantly compare them to other kids, outside or within the family. In effect, parents have to choose their kids again and again.
- Happiness: It is important for parents to be happy and to work at it. Parents need to demonstrate that being happy is not a given, nor is it the magic gift of external circumstances or tangible goods. It is created from within, every day, every hour. When it seems to be slipping away or events become overwhelming, parents have to teach their kids how to disengage, go quiet, take deep breaths, and tap into their resources to put Humpty Dumpty back together again. Above all, parents have to be vigilant and sensitive to reading

the signs of their kids' mood changes and be ready to intervene. Gently inquire about what seems to be off. If the response is that they do not wish to talk about it, that is a clear sign that eventually it has to be talked about. Don't second-guess and name what you think is wrong, because if you are right, your kid may not be willing to concede how transparent his need or situation is. With patience and trust on your part, your kids will tell you all. Above all, do not fall into the trap of telling your version of that experience when you were young. It will be resented as inappropriate and competitive. Also avoid minimizing the impact or scale of the problem. That trivializes what they are feeling and facing. Above all, do not rob them of their choices and decisions. Here is where Glasser's Choice Therapy comes to bear, and it also may be where parents perhaps can introduce relevant work experiences to suggest ways through to new, tougher, and more grown-up versions of happiness.

I hope many of you will try out the Parent Homework Journal (PHJ) and also put together a Code of Family Values. They both require effort on the part of parents, but the dividends may be well worth it. Besides, it should be considered parents' homework. Their grade will be their kids' happiness and school success, especially as they are reflected on the new report cards.

20

EARLY STARTS AND HEADS-UPS: SCHOOL, HOME, AND WORK

All parents follow a life cycle with their offspring that is both bonding and discontinuous, unifying and separating. They play out over time a series of evolving positions. At the beginning, they are indispensable. Babies and even toddlers cannot manage without them. Less intensely, that is so with pre-K and elementary school kids. With middle school if not sooner, parents and their offspring are more on a divergent than convergent course. With increasing independence, kids become more assertive, sassier, and private. The negative signal of that gradual separation is the anger of "Stop talking to me or treating me like a baby!" or, asked to help out and do some chores, "I am not your slave!"

Finally, by high school, conversation between parents and their kids is often labored and strained. Of course, they have no difficulty talking with their friends for hours, especially on the phone, but monosyllabic grunts may be their dominant responses to parents' questions. If they go away to college, the terrible silence of the empty nest syndrome suddenly descends. Parents look at each other in mutual bewilderment. Having invested so much of their own adult lives (and sometimes their unfulfilled dreams) in their kids, when they leave parents feel bereft, cut off, adrift. They appear to have lost their center and lifeline. If all they have talked about has been their kids, they may have little to say to each other, and they may not even be able to offer each other mutual consolation. Their time together now may be awkward and increasingly apart. They may develop separate interests, activities, and groups of friends. Occasional communication from their absent kids may spark and rekindle some bright or worried chatter about what is going on. They become parents again and talk.

PARALLEL LINES THAT ALMOST MEET

The specifics of the above double profile of parents and their kids and the dynamics of growing up and older obviously do not apply to all families. There are as many variations on the process as there are parts of the country and different cultures and belief systems that contribute to and shape those evolving relationships, but in all cases and to varying degrees nature and nurture are both involved and contribute their own distinct differences.

The nurture half of the equation is as deterministic a variable as its nature counterpart. The process follows a fixed evolutionary pattern: kids grow up, become increasingly independent, and leave home. They then form adult relationships and often have families, sometimes becoming clones of their own parents; and so the cycle repeats itself. However, the key point of this double evolutionary process is the absolute need for parents to anticipate and even begin to live a double future: that of their kids and of themselves.

Parents need to anticipate and prepare for the increasing independence not only of their kids, but also of themselves. Indeed, the argument here is that the more parents plan their own development as individuals and as husbands and wives, the better parents they will be. It is thus not a competitive but a complementary process. It shifts parents from being highly directive to primarily suggestive. While those role changes are going on, parental modeling of behavior, especially that of always looking ahead, may offer perhaps the most lasting influence. Before turning to kids and their changing needs, let us thus stay with the parents first.

PARENTS AND FAMILY WORK CONVERSATIONS

The most dramatic new sociology is the two-income family. Both parents are involved in family and work. In many middle-class homes, both salaries may be needed. In fact, economists rightly have suggested that this is precisely the way the middle class is currently remaining the middle class. Even when the mother or father elects to be a stay-at-home parent or homeschool their kids, the plan often is to return to work after the kids attend school full time. The practical needs of adult work schedules may explain why the majority of parents have raised little or no objection to increasing the length of the school day or the school year, including the elimination of the long summer vacation. San Diego just announced year-round schooling consisting of four major segments with two-week breaks in between. In short, working adults who are also parents (as well as, obviously, working single mothers or fathers) have an effect on their families and their cyclical relationships in many different ways.

By virtue of parents being more involved in their jobs, their conversations with each other and even their offspring may be ruled by work. Sometimes guilt occurs. Kids may object that they are locked out of the exchanges; besides, parents never talk about what interests them. How do parents handle this recurrent gap between working and schooling, between being a professional and a parent?

As in all things, balance is the answer, and sometimes a changing balance. When kids are infants or even toddlers, parents become accustomed to adult conversations. The problem is that they may become habitual. They may not be adjusted as the kids grow up and as the focus of the family shifts from work to school. Resentment or anger may be a wake-up call; or silence or withdrawal may be the telltale sign that something is off.

There are three key guidelines for parents, especially as kids get older:

1. Limit work conversations at home when kids are around. Reserve them for later exchanges between parents. Just as you need to pick your battles with kids, select what you talk about at home. Kids are ambiguous. They want you to leave them alone and not pester them, but they also want to believe that your lives are dedicated exclusively to them and not shared or absorbed by anything else or by others.

2. Replace work conversations with family conversations. Parents need to learn a new craft of managing family time and exchanges. In other chapters, we noted how families create rituals of celebrations,

discuss topics at dinner, grant initiatives to kids, rent movies and have popcorn or pizza together, and so on. In short, parents have to read the stages they and their kids are at in the evolutionary cycle and shift gears accordingly. Above all, it has to occur early.

3. But don't throw out the baby with the bathwater. Learn to extract from your work key elements that have generic interest and application. For example, a change in the evaluation system at work can be broadened to include kids' views of how they are evaluated, and what's good and bad about it. Another subject is the choices offered parents at work about professional development courses. Solicit their advice. What should be the basis of the choice? And how much choice do kids have in school? If you could design your own curriculum and day, what would it be like?

That last point needs to extended further.

COMMUNICATING THE CHANGING WORLD OF WORK

Much of what your kids will be encountering in the future is what working parents are experiencing now. In other words, if parents reflect on their own work experience they will see emerge the new patterns of jobs and careers that they can share with and use to guide their kids, but not in a heavy-handed or a punitive way by offering dire warnings of poverty or failure unless they do this or that. Such heavy-handed lecturing likely will fall on deaf ears. It may even backfire and produce the counterproductive response: "OK so I won't go to college. I will get a job as a plumber and make $28 an hour as an apprentice, and later $45 as a master." Then it escalates with the parental ultimatum: "If you want to ruin your life go ahead. Just make sure you buy enough of that special soap that removes the dirt under your fingernails!" Ironically, significant shortages of plumbers and others in the construction and skilled trades industries are expected.

What parents as workers who are experiencing changes now and in the future can provide their kids is a job basis for guiding student success. Five dominant and dominating patterns are emerging:

1. Organizations of all kinds and levels are absolutely insistent on employees having not only the basic skills of the three R's, but also organizational, time management, and problem solving skill sets, sometimes called Life or Study Skills. If parents set up the home as an operations center and process homework and test prep on a systematic mastery basis, they will be giving their kids the best basic foundation they will need for both school and work success.

2. Jobs and careers will change at least three to five times over the typical work lifetime, even that of the plumber. Many of those changes will be driven by technology and productivity. In the process, jobs may be eliminated, secretaries replaced by PCs, and live trainers by CD-ROMs. How do adults handle that? And what does it mean to kids who have not faced such disconnects? The answer is future basics: transition training and planning in terms of multiple talents and careers. Recall how the definitions of the eight or nine Multiple Intelligences (MI) were illustrated with their MOs—Multiple Occupations. Also, the planning exercise that involves kids using the road map of school choices from pre-K to college serves to introduce them not only to the value of planning, but also to the necessity always to keep alive their options and to invest future positioning with pivotal importance.

3. Traditional retirement and financial planning has taken on a new dimension. Adults are planning retirement careers, often in work areas totally different from what they did or are doing now. Such planning ahead also has served indirectly as a major psychological cushion or shock absorber to the empty nest syndrome. Some parents have created a double savings fund for their kids' college and for their retirement careers; and often when the kids decide not to go to college or to attend a less expensive state university, the one is channeled into the other. Much of the impetus for later-life planning is economic and medical: Social Security retirement eligibility shifting from sixty-two to seventy; general declines of workers' pensions; and greater longevity. Indeed, a new age category has been created in the latest census: a separate group of those over eighty-five now exists to reflect changing demographics. Everyone under that age is considered younger. It is important for parents who are contemplating retirement careers, especially those that

involve significant changes of where one lives and what kind of home one chooses, to share that decision with their kids and to solicit their input. It not only alerts and conveys to kids a work and life pattern that likely will also affect them, but demonstrates that their wishes and future lives still are intertwined, and that wherever possible their views will be factored in.

4. Competition will reign supreme, especially that brought about by the global economy. Until we can understand why the insurance industry reroutes its customer service calls to operators in Ireland, or Dell to technicians in India, and why airlines offer incentives to book online or use e-ticket kiosks to reduce the number of reservation employees, we will not fully understand the intensity of global competition and why the emphasis on worker productivity drives the increased use of technology and downsizing. How can this new reality be conveyed to kids? By talking about competition in school—by asking about the effects of tests and why or whether we should have them, and by discussing the selection admissions policies of some colleges and what they are based on, and so on. Above all, encourage them to explore all options—let them come to independent and discovered notions of competition. Don't steal their decisions and discoveries from them.

5. Diversity, including global diversity, now rules. Opportunities are no longer gender determined. Girls do not have to be nurses; they can be doctors. They do not have to be teachers; they can be principals. In addition, Caucasians in some parts of the U.S. and the workforce, and certainly in the world, are no longer the majority; just as Christianity may globally no longer be the dominant religion of the world. Study abroad programs, previously reserved only for the few or the wealthy, are now increasingly a standard option for many college students. In short, the twenty-first century is a new world that parents already are experiencing in part and that their kids will encounter totally. The more parents can expose them to diversity, the better prepared they will be to live with competition and choice as norms of both school and work. Above all, it will help them to manage the tough complexity of working their way through commonality and differentiation. The standard notions are: everyone deep down is the same, or everyone essentially

is different. The composite perhaps houses the truth: everyone is the same, differently. Constantly negotiating and renegotiating that synthesis is a lifelong task that both parents and kids have to share. Moreover, parents need to allow kids their own space, not only for independent discovery, but also for role reversal. The kids may parent the parents.

Creating and structuring family time together and crafting family conversations are all part of what parents can do to guide their kids to student success. But there are also a number of other interventions and intersects, many basic, that are inevitably tied to chronological development.

EARLY STARTS

Everything seems to be occurring sooner rather than later. Some proactive parents at the birth of their kids enroll them in popular nursery schools or even later in kindergartens that have waiting lists. However, such planning ahead should not obscure two basics. First, kids have to be regularly checked out and checked upon physically. Second, from birth to age three, all kids are being homeschooled.

The physical basics include not only the predictable inoculations, but also eyes, ears, and motor development. It is important for vision and hearing to be checked as soon as it is sensible to do so. Kentucky two years ago mandated an optical exam for all first graders. More than 30 percent needed corrective glasses. Imagine what those kids would have missed for the next two to three years? Hearing also needs to be checked early; problems there will affect speech development. Finally, parents need to pay attention to motor control—to muscle and limb development. Often some congenital problems, such as vertical talus (inverted arches), are not picked up at birth. Pediatrics has now become a diverse series of specializations: orthopedic, neurological, and so on. They are the ones to allay or confirm your suspicions.

New parents tend to be understandably anxious. Some have even claimed that is why the first child often turns out to be an overachiever. Aside from counting the number of fingers and toes at birth, the later focus is just as intense. It all revolves around the question, "Is my kid normal?"—which means usually when he begins to crawl or says his first word or discovers his nose. The problem here is time—not whether, but when. Because each stage is not a precise point but a range, and because all kids are different and evolve at different rates, the major reassurance that parents routinely have to be given is that almost all kids ultimately reach the same end points, and that those who do so earlier have no edge over those who do so later. But in the second basic area, that of learning behaviors at home, observation and early detection are crucial.

BASIC LEARNING BEHAVIORS, AGES 2–7

The reason for paying knowledgeable attention to kids during the early years is that when corrective action is indicated, it can rapidly be taken, bring about immediate change, and prevent later learning problems. Experts on the subject have found that unfortunately the majority of learning problems are not detected until the ages of eleven to twelve, and then many not until the age of seventeen. Some parents often deny that anything is amiss, that he will catch up later, have a growth spurt in intelligence, that his older brother was also a late bloomer, that he will outgrow it, and so on. But what happens if all these explanations do not pan out, and valuable time meanwhile has been lost?

Parents are in a unique position to make a series of key diagnostic decisions because in effect every kid from birth to preschool is being homeschooled. Parents teach, observe, and evaluate development, but parents in turn need guidance.

The problem with providing a checklist of age-appropriate learning behaviors is that often they are used solely as an early warning system. Aside from contributing to parental anxiety and even paranoia, the truth is they also should be used as an early opportunity system. They should be in effect the curriculum of the early home school. Thus what follows below is a learning behaviors checklist organized by ages but cast in positive form for parents to employ. Opportunities to evaluate performance also have been provided, with the cautionary note that only when the number of questions or issues far outweighs the number of achievements might there be cause for concern.

Preschool: 2–5 Years Old

Learning Behavior Activities   OK   Questions/Issues
1. Enjoys playing sound games.
2. Likes repetition and rhyming.
3. Rejects baby talk.
4. Favors grown-up words.
5. Recognizes letters of his name.
6. Remembers numbers and days of the week.

Kindergarteners: 5–6 Years Old

1. Able to write letters.
2. Can write his name.
3. Recognizes words that rhyme.
4. Connects letters with sounds.
5. Can relate words with the same sound.
6. Keeps parts of words together (like cowboy).

First Graders: 6–7 Years Old

1. Reads more than one-syllable words.
2. Connects sounds and letters while reading.
3. Recognizes irregularly spelled words.
4. Enjoys reading.
5. Happy to read to others.

Second and Later Grades: 7–9 Years Old

1. Pronounces complicated words.
2. Is not confused by soundalike words.
3. Speaks clearly.
4. Has a good vocabulary.
5. Avoids calling everything stuff.
6. Remembers dates, names, and phone numbers.
7. Does not skip or lose place.
8. Spells well.

9. Has neat handwriting.
10. Completes homework.
11. Finishes tests.

Parents have much to give, especially in the early years. As noted earlier they are the child's first teachers and the home is the first school. It
should be a place of success. It should be a place where the foundations
of self-esteem are established and where play and learning are the same
thing. In addition to being a reassuring and happy place, it is also
uniquely an enriching and experimenting place. It is there where MI
can be tried out, where learning may be given many new leases on life,
and where new worlds and horizons appear to expand a child's learning
parameters. In fact, as we have noted, if it does not happen at home it
may not happen in school. In short, the home and parents offer the
learning insurance of alternative ways. Otherwise all the eggs are placed
solely in the school basket, and the stakes are too high to deny the home
a key role. Parents are just too important—all the time: early, later on,
and always.

21

NEW REPORT CARDS AND SYSTEMS

Education is currently on a fast track of add-ons and incremental overlays. All curricula now need to be amplified and multidirectional. Minimally, they thus need to be differentiated, assessment-driven, research-based, cognitively focused, and character-directed. Optimally, they should apply the principles of multiple intelligence. Whatever the variations, assessment has now become so all-encompassing (some would say omnipresent) that the measurement of curricula has become a separate growth industry. It even has generated new administrative career tracks and positions. Currently, it appears to have become more important, urgent, and intrusive than curricula development.

Given such pressures for accountability, it was perhaps inevitable that the way performance results should be displayed and communicated to students and parents would become the next logical stage for review, reconfiguration, and revision. To be sure, most attention has been paid to the larger public issues of school district report cards and the display of individual schools needing improvement according to NCLB guidelines. However, there is another related report process going on, which, although spawned by the same pressures of national accountability, is taking on a life and importance of its own: individual report cards of students.

This perhaps unexpected development is part and parcel of implementing systems of learning metrics. To track, document, report, and evaluate school, teacher, and student performance, many school districts have installed complex electronic monitoring systems. They are busily printing out performance data profiles on a weekly or monthly basis. They usually use sophisticated software capable of disaggregating on a student-by-student basis subject areas and state test scores. Purchased from vendors who promised full display capability and even teacher-friendly adaptability, educators suddenly have found that such data could become the grist for the mill of individual student report cards.

A few school districts jumped on the bandwagon early on. Not to be outdone, the New York City school system, after years of planning and testing, recently developed a report card that was twelve pages long. Within months of introducing that new amplified version, Joe Klein, the head of the system, scrapped that cumbersome version for a streamlined four-page version. More recently, the Seattle school district issued a new report card, interestingly also four pages long (*Seattle Post-Intelligencer* 2003). Although the examples are few and the research on applications limited, clearly administrators are being asked to apply their instructional leadership to this new offspring of assessment and to managing the cornucopia of data.

Examining the general guidelines administrators have to follow in the development of a new report card, or more accurately a new reporting system, may reveal much about the rationale and the process. Six areas have been identified:

THE BASICS

1. Planning Time: Complexity and feedback require administrators to allow at least two years to develop a draft and to solicit feedback from teachers, parents, students, and other administrators.
2. Focus: Consider grade span. Although all current report card revisions typically start with elementary schools, there is nothing sacred or absolute about that. In fact, given exit exams for graduation, a good argument can be made for starting with high school.

3. Testing: Use students to try out the drafts. First, the report card itself thus can be a learning experience; evaluation, especially self-
evaluation, is an important part of instruction. Second, it reorgan-
izes students' thinking about managing their learning in general
and about the designated improvement strategies in particular. In
short, it hopefully makes them more reflective students. Third,
they can explain the complexities to their bewildered parents.

4. Computerized Forms: Use computerized forms for this complex
task, which, though time-consuming, can still be more efficient than
hand entry. The downside is the loss of individual handwritten notes,
but those can be communicated in follow-up teacher conferences.

5. Displays, Footnotes, and Legends: Manage the complexity of
content and detail. Visual communications must rule. An initial
at-a-glance survey must provide the overall picture and motivate
more in-depth examination. Avoid jargon. If grade indicators are
being changed from ABCDF to a numerical or other system, explain why. Anticipate questions about transfers to other school
districts (including those outsides of the state) and acceptance by
college admissions. Append a document that explains alignment
of federal, state, and local standards and provides a glossary or
legend. Give websites that explore NCLB in detail.

6. Multiple Measures: Introduce the rationale for multiple measures
and the complexity of managing complexity. Each subject is multiply
assessed in at least five areas. In math for example, two might include
"defines and solves problems" and "uses mathematical reasoning."
Then each of these five areas in turn would be broken down into five
subset areas, such as "collects, organizes, and displays data appropriately." The net result is a total of nine measurements benchmarked
in math alone or a total of almost fifty indicators. Finally, attention
should be paid to offering summative measurements, which, like
subtotals, reflect a fourfold performance range, such as beginning,
approaching standard, standard, and above-standard levels.

AUDIENCES

Nuts-and-bolts issues must be accompanied by addressing the concerns
and expectations of at least three constituencies.

1. All teachers have to be brought on board. This is not an optional activity or limited to some, but an across-the-board template for the entire district. Obviously, professional development sessions on assessing data and critically evaluating student work tied to new reporting formats would be enormously critical. Indeed, the new report card may hasten and even anchor the new commitment to data tracking and above all to assessment.

2. Students need to see its diagnostic and corrective value. Whatever generic explanations are offered, for the process to take hold it must be applied in every subject area in every class via learning rubrics. In some cases, students may even be given separate grades for each rubric development line with a summary average provided. Above all, students must be persuaded that this new report card is fair, comprehensive, and individualistic. It is not only a more accurate reflection of what they are doing and where they are at, but also a mental map of who they are.

3. Ultimately, parents should find this new report card clarifying. They may see in the measurement of their own kids the specific results and applications of the changes that have occurred in educational requirements and reporting that now affect all schools. Local standards are now shaped by national and state performance standards. What also needs to be underscored are the serious consequences for their schools and their kids if local schools do not make a good-faith effort to comply with NCLB. Above all, parents need to discern how this new report card can better guide, focus, and increase their own intervention and involvement. Indeed, one of the critical side goals is to use the new report card to build stronger partnerships between teachers and parents.

RATIONALE

Finally, all designers of the new report card and their constituencies need to be on the same page as to why this is being done, what the goals are, and what strategies make good sense to use:

1. Catch-up: In many ways the new report card is a way of updating everyone on current educational practice. It is a way for everyone

involved to catch up with all the changes and all be on the same page, together.

2. Line Up: Alignment rules. It runs from the individual school to the district to the state to the federal levels. Goals and testing have to be all in synch.

3. Leg Up: The aim is to improve student performance. Slippage is identified, areas of improvement disaggregated for focused intervention, and finally corrective action recommended as a leg up for improvement. Diagnosis is regularly paired with intervention.

4. Step Up: However, action and commitment are required by all constituencies, acting in concert. Each is different but all require the collective decision to step up to the plate and bring about reinforced change over time and on task.

5. Heads Up: This is anticipatory. Without being melodramatic, this can serve as an early warning system alerting students and parents of what is coming down the pike during the rest of the school year and in the years ahead, subject by subject. Here is where the larger picture is drawn and the macro and the micro are linked in a moving timeline. Students steadily losing ground or going up a down escalator may not be able to recoup lost ground without major interventions of tutoring and/or summer school. This dimension of the new report card, although the most speculative, may turn out to be the most effective motivator for change. A road map of the future and its branch points may provide the right dramatization of long-range plans that parents especially may value.

ADDING BELLS AND WHISTLES

Inevitably, some school districts that are more technological and/or student- and parent-centered may wish to expand the document. Some variations might include the following:

1. Multimedia: The new report card may provide and encourage electronic access to student portfolios and videos as enriched supplements to the basic categories. This additional resource might even go further in displaying and documenting graphically the

learning attitudes, styles, and multiple intelligences of students than the most elaborate written comments of teachers.

2. Student-Led: The follow-up to the distribution of the new report card can be the parent–teacher conference. However, consideration should be given to one that is student-led, with the student having been trained to lead the discussion and to discuss his take on the grades on the report card.

3. Parental Follow-up: The report card may be used to develop an additional printout of parental assignments and resources. The home would then be joined with the classroom in a reinforced effort. The new report card should be regarded and used as an optimum vehicle not only for increasing parental involvement in general, but also in specific, focused, and even prescriptive ways. Teachers would thus be able to add a key learning partner to jointly help meet higher standards.

WIDER ISSUES

It is important to view the opportunity of creating a new report card as more than a mechanical exercise. Minimally, it brings together a number of critical issues.

1. It joins together and upgrades state-of-the-art assessment with communications technology. Designing the report card may even lead back to improving the assessment system itself that generates the data.

2. It provides the occasion to revisit the extent to which the school is really student-centered and to consider whether it also should be student-led.

3. Finally, it invests with great importance the value of parental involvement to the point where teachers and parents have to work together and develop specific learning plans that are jointly undertaken.

The new report card above all will belong to parents and their kids.

Part 6

COMING ATTRACTIONS

Although this parental guide has sought primarily to engage current realities, it also has tried to anticipate some future developments. Above all, it has urged parents to adopt a proactive planning mode. However, given the general pace and impact of change, today's table of contents may be radically altered over the time span of your kids' growing up. In that case, even speculation of what may be coming down the pike might be welcome.

A crystal ball is not needed to recognize the major transformations of K–16 education. Three megaforces will parallel and even converge with each other. The first already has appeared, NCLB, although according to the most recent Gallup Poll, almost 75 percent of parents are not familiar with its requirements. The appearance and implementation of such National Standards will be joined by the gradual surfacing and acceptance of National Curriculum Models.

These will emerge gradually. They will be tested over time, and found to be deserving of national nomination because they satisfy the most comprehensive criteria. They will be research-based, incorporate the latest brain findings, minister to differentiated and diverse populations, and enable students to pass mandated tests. The competition for which ones will be the National Models and serve as the keys to heaven will be intense and partisan.

Finally, the conjoined needs for economic viability and political de-centralization will both gradually and radically alter the way schools are organized and operate, especially large urban districts. Top-heavy and expensive layers will be replaced by granting direct control and self-determinism at the individual school level. Such political governance will involve total fiscal management and accountability. No more will educators be able to blame the System; or as Pogo noted: "We have met the enemy and he is us."

The overall impact of these three megaforces will be to intensify the contest and the debate between national needs and goals, and individual and local self-determination and freedom—in short, between Big Brother and the Rugged Pioneer and Innovative Entrepreneur. What and who will finally win? Judging by our history, all will; and we will learn to live with and negotiate yet another compromise and definition of the American culture and character.

What appears below as the final chapter is a less dramatic and comprehensive, but no less important, series of future probes directed at educational areas that are likely to undergo major transformations between 2005 and 2025. This heads-up for parents is intended to serve not so much as an early warning as an early opportunity system. With this outline of probable future developments in hand, parents in effect can update this guide. They can thus continue to provide their kids with the kind of guidance and interventions that will enable them not only to live that new future, but also help to create it.

22

CONCLUSION: TEN DRIVING TRENDS

Ten future developments will have a major impact on education during the first quarter of the twenty-first century:

I. TECHNOLOGY

By 2025 significant segments of education will be delivered electronically. It will begin in nursery school and at home with learning robots: every student will have one. As much as one-half of learning will be computer driven. Some high school students will take all their courses online; they will never set foot into an actual school building but function virtually. Microsoft just entered into a partnership with the Philadelphia school system to design a $45 million state-of-the-art electronic learning center. It undoubtedly is intended to serve as a model for replication by other school systems. Then, too, the interaction of economics and national standards will leverage the emergence of the technology-amplified teacher and tutor. Parents need to become technology literate if they are to continue to provide support for their kids' success.

2. TIME AND PLACE: ARCHITECTURE AND STRUCTURE

The school year and the school day will be extended. Year-round schooling may become the national norm. The school day will start early and end late. Following the lead of California, states also will provide free preschool opportunities for all children. Head Start will be universal. Successful experiments with public boarding schools for kids from broken or dysfunctional homes may lead to their wide-scale adoption, especially in urban and rural areas. As a counterreaction to the extended year and day, more families may elect homeschooling. If a tax credit to cover some of the costs of homeschooling is provided, enrollments will accelerate. Parents may have to rethink their own schedules as well as the after-school activities of their kids. The critical issue that parents may wish to address is what is being planned and scheduled by schools for that extra time.

3. NATURE VIA NURTURE

The classic debate and opposition between genetics and environment will experience convergence. Not only will both be acknowledged as equal partners, but their relations will be interoperable. Genetics will be found to be influenced by environment and environment will be found to be affected by genetics. The genetic profile of each child will help not only to shape the school and home environment, but to optimize and to some extent modify the ways that environment can alter genetics. Every school will have genetic environmentalist counselors on its staff. They will work with both teachers and parents, consulting on the designs of the school and home environments respectively. In effect what may emerge is a new science and psychology of predicting potential. Parents will thus become advocates of those environments that contribute to the maximum or optimum realization of that potential.

4. BRAIN RESEARCH

By 2025 if not sooner the entire brain will be mapped. A new breed of cognitive psychologists will be able to chart scientifically all the learning pathways, and curricula and support materials will be redesigned accordingly. All new teachers will be given courses in brain research; current staff, professional development workshops. Allied with computer specialists, cognitive psychologists will develop artificial intelligence to the point where it may rival human intelligence. Kids in the future will be symbiotic: an alignment or fusion of human and machine intelligence. Parents may have to become increasingly comfortable with science fiction.

5. MULTIPLE INTELLIGENCES

There will be greater acceptance of Gardner's MI as an accurate and comprehensive system of knowing and developing. The eight basic avenues may attain the status of Maslov's hierarchy or, more precisely, express for the first time the fullest expression of the notion of self-actualization. In any case, MI will become the driving force behind differentiated education and rubric definitions in school. Even with extended school days, the home will have to take up the slack. Parents will have to individualize the enrichment and enhancement of MIs not available or provided for in school. Above all, MI will become the preferred child-rearing instructional methodology from birth to preschool.

6. TRANSITION TRAINING AND SCHOOLING

The pace and invasiveness of change will be intense. The projection is that during the first three decades of the twenty-first century, the equivalent of 20,000 years of progress will be introduced. The issue of coping will surface even for kids, for whom the rate of change generally is more manageable. What is likely to appear is in effect a new adaptability to transience, which will be based on a revised understanding of the nature of transition. The typical view is that transition is a necessary but stressful interlude between one previously stable situation and one that lies ahead. However, the transition is being followed instead by another transition and that by another and so on. The net result is that transition becomes not the exception but the norm.

Transition becomes permanent. Some professionals and all futurists already operate on those assumptions of an altered reality; but students need to be reoriented to transition as a permanent norm if they are to function effectively in school and later in work. Parents also will need the same transition training if they are to stay on top of all that is changing and affecting their kids' future and remain sane and in control.

7. EDUCATIONAL LEADERSHIP AND MANAGEMENT: LEADERSHIP SHARING

The traditional focus on the single or primary leader will change radically. Where principals remain visible, there will be extensive leadership sharing with teachers and staff. In some schools, as already has happened in the McCosh elementary school in Chicago and elsewhere, teacher councils run the school. In a dozen charter schools in Minnesota, the Ed/Visions cooperative, teachers have replaced principals but remained in the classroom. They are teacher leaders. Parents have to remain politically vigilant and fill the power vacuum by becoming a significant player in the general leadership sharing; otherwise, they will be left out and the educational and advocacy agenda of parents may be lost in the shuffle.

8. TEAM AND COLLABORATIVE LEARNING

Typically, the major developmental stages of youth have been from dependence to independence. The future will require a third stage, interdependence. Increasingly, teachers and students will work in teams and be team members, teachers, and leaders. In schools where there is extensive leadership sharing, teams will run the schools. In schools where principals have been replaced by teacher leaders, governance will be totally collaborative. Correspondingly, students will be placed in learning groups or teams, especially if the current five-day schedule of classes and subjects is downshifted to three, with the slack being taken up with student study teams. Instead of play dates, parents may have to facilitate study dates. Taking turns, parents may have to invite over and form study groups in their homes especially focused on test prep. If the school has failed to provide instruction on team dynamics and conflict resolution, parents may have to stand by as moderators. Perhaps the best affirmation of cooperative learning is Blanchard's statement: "None of us is as smart as all of us."

9. ECONOMICS OF SCHOOL REFORM

Charter schools, unlike public schools, in effect operate with a bottom line. All are involved in shaping and maintaining the budget. If they consistently operate in the red they close, unlike traditional public schools, which are bailed out by the district. In other words, the current accountability movement has not included to date but will insist on fiscal accountability. Annual increases each year requiring increases in taxes will be accompanied by new cost controls. The budgets of some school districts will be reduced, and schools will be required collectively to manage their own fiscal affairs. Those that don't will, as NCLB requires, be closed, taken over, or be restructured. Parents will play pivotal roles. As professionals in their own right, many parents can offer fiscal husbandry. Some may reduce costs by serving as unpaid volunteers. Most importantly, they will expand their historical role of providing financial support, but now and in the future it will take the form of establishing legal and separate nonprofit foundations. Such extraschool arrangements in effect will enable parents to apply the economic leverage to support their advocacy agenda.

10. JOB/CAREER AND LEAPFROGGING OPTIONS

No Child Left Behind is more of a political promise than it is a realizable goal. A more honest and accurate statement is fewer children left behind. Given the heavy emphasis on testing, inevitably some will be. The question is, how many? And what if anything will be done for them? We already have part of the answer as to numbers. In Florida 4,000 kids who failed the third-grade reading and math tests are scheduled to be left behind and to repeat the third grade. In Massachusetts about 6,000 seniors failed the high school exit exam and thus were denied a high school diploma, the minimum passport to even the most menial jobs. It has happened elsewhere to great consternation. Colleges that already had accepted these youngsters indicated they would honor their enrollment. Many states and school districts quickly changed the dates of implementing the graduation exam to three to five years later. California just announced that it is postponing the test date to 2006. Obviously, heavy test prep would be directed in the interim to avoid large-scale failures, although in the case of Massachusetts all who failed had taken the test five times, the maximum allowed. In short, the issue is, how much such failure is attributable to so called unteachable kids and how much to the school's inability to structure alternatives?

Once again embarrassment rather than enlightenment may force a change. The numbers failing will remain high. Given chronic academic failure, beginning in elementary school (what William Glasser described and predicted), combined with the elimination of social promotion, the conventional ways of turnaround may be replaced by two radical solutions, both partly visible today. Job training will replace traditional academic education as an option for some students. In Philadelphia job academies have been set up as part of regular high schools. One devoted to the restaurant and hospitality industry attracted the Outback chain, which built a regular functioning restaurant open to the public as part of the high school. Students will be trained in all aspects of the job, and when they graduate each will become manager of an Outback restaurant.

A more ambitious innovation already has been tried with success with at-risk kids in Oakland, California. The kids are being offered college-level classes early in the morning, before regular high school starts. The enrollment has been strong and students persist. Dropout rates have fallen dramatically, and many have graduated and gone to college. In fact, open enrollment community colleges frequently accept high school dropouts because they often do well, especially in classes where the students are older, hold down jobs, and are serious. Parents of kids who might benefit by being offered such alternatives need to lobby for such changes. It makes no sense to persist with a system that passes school failure onto society and job failure and offers little or no hope to those who have not been able to make it in particular. If the schools can't see that, the parents of those kids certainly can; and they need to be listened to.

PARTING WORDS AND WISHES

Parent–teacher relationships and conferences will be invested with greater importance and value in the future. That will be driven by the increasing recognition that the school will not be able to achieve its performance goals, let alone have them last, without parental involvement. Another compelling factor is that new report cards will emerge. They will capture and display all the detailed and complex findings of the data tracking systems put in place to honor accountability. The net result is that parent–teacher conferences will be more balanced. Evaluation will become a shared rather than a unilateral exchange. That in turn also will accommodate parent input in general about their kids' learning and thinking styles and multiple intelligences, as revealed at home and during homework, as well their involvement and performance in after-school and weekend activities. In short, parents will be quick to seize on new developments in reporting and higher standards to become advocates of 360-degree evaluation. That way their kids will have the benefit of being at the center of a series of multiple inputs, perspectives, intelligences, and above all, choices.

The shift from control to coordination, from unilateral directive instruction to collaborative inquiry, will drive the preference for learning that integrates curricula and student choice. National models that do not have to choose between short-term test mastery and long-term cognitive growth, between assessment and investment, will engage increasingly the advocacy of both teachers and parents. Glasser's basic antidotes to coercion and school failure, quality and choice, will take hold and produce quality schools, teachers, and parents. In short, all that is needed is known and available. It just needs leadership.

The entire thrust of this guide is that parents will be the leaders of the future. In a sense they have to be. They are the only ones for whom the future is real, personal, and urgent. It appears in their kids, and the stakes are high and getting tougher.

Parent leadership will take many forms. For some it will focus on the home and shaping family structures, times, rituals, and conversations to build self-confidence and student success. For others it will emphasize building two-way and reciprocal relationships between teachers and parents and bringing school and home closer together and more in synch. For a smaller number it may involve larger leadership roles with the PTA or school boards advocating school reform. Or the options may change or be combined as their kids do and as circumstances alter; but whatever role parents choose, hopefully all will recognize that they have no other choice but that of leadership.

Given the intensity and intelligence of such parental advocacy, instead of writing "The End" for this book, parents should write

The Beginning!

WORKS CITED

Armstrong, Thomas. *The Multiple Intelligences of Reading and Writing: Making the Words Come Alive.* Alexandria, Va.: Association for Supervision and Curriculum Development, 2003.

Deming, W. Edwards. *The New Economics for Industry, Government, Education.* Cambridge, Mass.: MIT, 1993.

"Education Reform." *Seattle Post-Intelligencer.* April 12, 2003, p. 24.

Gardner, Howard. *Frames of Mind: The Theory of Multiple Intelligences.* New York: Basic Books, 1983.

Glasser, William. *The Quality School: Managing Students without Coercion.* New York: Harper, 1998.

Hammer, Michael, and James Champy. *Reengineering the Corporation: A Manifesto for Business Revolution.* New York: HarperBusiness, 1993.

Jarger, Arnold. "In Search of Reform." *Education Week* 12 (January 21, 2001).

Lambert, Linda. *Leadership Capacity for Lasting School Improvement.* Alexandria, Va.: Association for Supervision and Curriculum Development, 2003.

Ouchi, William. "Teacher Quality." *Education Week* 44 (September 6, 2003).

Sobelly, Thomas. "In Search of Superintendents, A Dearth of Thinking Outside the Box." *Education Week* 124 (December 13, 2001).

ABOUT THE AUTHOR

Irving H. Buchen secured his Ph.D. from The Johns Hopkins University and has taught and served as an administrator at California State University, University of Wisconsin, and Penn State. He currently is vice president of academic affairs of Aspen University and a member of the doctoral faculty of Capella University, both distance education institutions. He is also an active management and education consultant. He is a Senior Research Associate with Comwell, HR Partners, and Ed/Visions, and is CEO of his own training and coaching company offering parent success workshops nationally and internationally. An active researcher, he has published four books (soon to be five) and over 150 articles. He can be reached at ibuchen@msn.com.